THE FACE IN THE MIЯROR

THE FACE IN THE MIЯROR

*WRITERS REFLECT
ON THEIR
DREAMS OF YOUTH
AND THE
REALITY OF AGE*

EDITED BY VICTORIA ZACKHEIM

Prometheus Books

59 John Glenn Drive
Amherst, New York 14228–2119

Published 2009 by Prometheus Books

"God Bless the Child," written by Billie Holiday and Arthur Herzog Jr.,
used by permission of Edward B. Marks Music Company.

Inquiries should be addressed to
Prometheus Books
59 John Glenn Drive
Amherst, New York 14228–2119
VOICE: 716–691–0133, ext. 210
FAX: 716–691–0137
WWW.PROMETHEUSBOOKS.COM

13 12 11 10 09   5 4 3 2

Library of Congress Cataloging-in-Publication Data

Zackheim, Victoria.
    The face in the mirror : writers reflect on their dreams of youth and the reality of age / edited by Victoria Zackheim.
        p. cm.
    ISBN 978–1–59102–752–2 (hardcover : alk. paper)
    1. Authors, American—Biography. 2. Self-perception in authors.
3. Adolescence. 4. Ambition. 5. Experience.

PS129 .F26 2009
810.9/005 B 22

2009016312

Printed in the United States of America on acid-free paper

For *Jill Marsal*

CONTENTS

INTRODUCTION

When you were in your youth—riding your bicycle, playing stickball, learning how to knit, sitting too close to that old black-and-white television, attending the senior prom—did you look in the mirror and imagine yourself in any way close to the person you are today? And now that you are here, in this place, at this age, do you look back with longing at the old dreams and expectations? Perhaps you are delighted, even surprised, by what you have achieved.

In my adolescence, the child I saw in that

mirror in no way resembled the person I've become, and I imagine many of us can say the same. You wanted to be a doctor or ballerina, the next person to walk on the moon, a teacher who stirs the imagination of students. Did those dreams come true? Perhaps a more important question: Was your future defined by your own dreams or by the dreams and expectations of others? Some authors in this collection were encouraged by the people in their lives, while others have succeeded despite them.

Whether we like it or not, we live in a society that gauges its citizens not by the content of our dreams but by the accomplishments in our careers. There's a presumption that successful people—that is, people who earn an excellent living or get mentioned in the newspaper from time to time—must certainly feel satisfied, even exhilarated, for having achieved so much. In many cases, I'm sure this is true. But maybe a question we need to ask ourselves is, What is our own gauge for success? If we could answer this, we might understand why some of us set the bar so low, demanding little of ourselves and waiting to see what happens, while others aim unrealistically high.

More than a few authors in this collection write about the desire to achieve, as well as those obstacles that hindered their journey: unexpected parenthood, family pressures, economic need, emotional trauma. In Alan Dershowitz's poignant and sometimes hilarious essay, we learn that he had high personal expectations, yet his family and teachers saw little academic future for the boy and urged him toward successful mediocrity. Eileen Goudge writes about being a divorced mother on welfare at the age of twenty-one. It took discipline, a borrowed typewriter, and the ability to avert her eyes from her landlord flasher, but she sat down and wrote. Today, more than five million of her books are in print worldwide, many of them *New York Times* best sellers.

Numerous writers in this collection attained success in midlife, but one did so as a teenager. Joyce Maynard was a college freshman when the *New York Times Magazine* published her article "An Eighteen-Year-Old Looks Back on Life," launching her as one of the country's top authors. But what happened when, decades later, she found herself grown, the mother of three adult children, and sitting across from a much younger man who was clearly attracted to her?

There are so many variables that affect how successful we become. One of the most powerful is that of family. It is no secret that a happy family, encouraging parents, and a carefree childhood are strong foundations for a healthy adult life. A few of the contributors enjoyed that gift, while others did not. Writer and psychotherapist Margot Duxler discloses how her recovery from childhood abuse led her into a life of caregiving, beginning with the adoption of a teenage girl when Margot was still in her twenties.

Few authors today write about family and courage with more insight and humor than Christine O'Hagan. In her essay, we learn about a challenging youth made bearable by the hilarious, beyond-fiction characters who populated her world; a memoir waiting to happen. When she married and had children, it was this same insight and biting Irish humor put to the page that guided her through a tragedy no mother should have to bear.

How many of us grew up swearing to ourselves that we would never become our parents? It seems to be one of life's dirty little tricks that it happens nevertheless. Do we accept this with maturity—even relief, if we come to the realization that Mom and Dad were not, as we once thought, Satan incarnate—and embrace the similarities? Sandra Gulland rose from the antiwar sit-ins of Berkeley's wild '60s to a woman centered and at peace, now writing best-selling historical novels about turbulent eras of the past. At the same time, she is ever aware of her own history and increasingly aware of how much it has been shaped by her mother: her tastes, her passions, her love of words. "We become our parent," she writes, reminiscing with tenderness about her mother's final days and the time they spent together. "How can it be otherwise?"

Whether we mature into replicas of our parents or forge a path—emotionally, spiritually, socially—that takes us in unique and unexpected directions, we somehow learn to live with the disappointment of dreams unfulfilled. But what happens when we work toward some distant and seemingly unattainable goal, and then reach it? Does this give us the happiness and fulfillment we expected? For those who became the corporate CEO but whose secret dream was to be a Super Bowl–winning quarterback, success might be both sweet and bitter. This dichotomy between reality and fantasy, in the form of childhood yearnings unfulfilled, is explored in several of the essays in this book. You'll discover that while most of the authors valued their adult accomplishments, there was nevertheless that crucial moment when the little voice whispering *ballet dancer*, *talk show host*, *batting champion* was forever silenced.

Perhaps there are as many reasons why our goals are not met—illness, war, hardship, family obligations—as there are ways to leap those barriers and find success. I wonder how many of us developed *Plan A* for our lives and suddenly realized we were living *Plan B* . . . and it was wonderful. Your company downsized, then you found your dream job; your marriage failed, and you met the love of your life. Reading these authors, you'll be reminded how so many of us are thrilled by the unexpected direction life often takes. Being given a second, or a third, or even a fourth chance doesn't mean we've failed. It means we have the opportunity to live our life infused with a vibrancy and purpose we hardly dared to anticipate.

Years ago, I met a man whose specialty was putting together funding for Silicon Valley start-ups. When the funds were in place, he would take on the role of chief financial officer and stay with the company until it was ready to fly. Once it launched, he would resign his position and look for the next start-up, taking with him substantial shares of stock. He did this for nearly five years, amassing a considerable fortune along the way. One day, his mother called. She was in her eighties, and her voice quivered as she expressed her concerns about her son's life. "But I'm doing great!" he enthused. After a long silence, his mother responded, "You say so, dear, but you never seem to be able to hold a job." He was a risk taker, his mother was a child of the Depression, and his sense of adventure and joy caused her untold anxiety, perhaps because, like so many of us, he was living his dreams, not hers.

There is a thread that runs through this book, and it is the expression of a sense of completeness, of being whole. In many ways, this relates to the importance of learning to live in our skin, of becoming comfortable with who we are. Feeling complete, knowing ourselves, opens the door to creativity and risk taking. You might be surprised to discover that it's not fame that led many of these writers to this place, but their ability to transform that surprising journey we call *life* into an adventure. Few journeys from obscurity to celebrity are as dramatic as that of Beverly Donofrio, who went from being a teenage mother to a convicted felon, and then college student to notable author. Now living in a monastery in the Colorado mountains, she reveals with humor and poignancy what led her to this place of peace and forgiving.

As important as it is to forgive ourselves, we must also forgive others. Michael Bader explores this challenge through his experience at his father's deathbed. The journey he took toward resolution with a man he loved and admired, and for whom he also felt great disappointment and resentment, reminds us that forgiveness may not be as powerful as the ability to let go.

In these pages, celebrated authors tackle universal questions about the choices they made and the achievements and disappointments that followed. They explore the person they expected to become, the person they perhaps desperately wanted to be—or feared they might be—and the person they are today. Their essays run the gamut of personal reflection, from exalting at having lived a long and productive life, to feeling that they have yet to reach their goals. Malachy McCourt shares his hardscrabble life in Limerick, as frightening as it was suffocating. How did he survive? Perhaps it was his philosophy: "If you want to give God a good laugh, tell Him your future plans."

However the authors view their lives or approach their personal revelations in this book, and whether their essays are funny or poignant, wicked or thought provoking, the heart of this anthology beats around one prevailing question: *When you look in the mirror, who do you see?*

AL GIESE

CHARLES DRUCKER

BECOMING INTERNATIONAL

Aimee Liu

When I was a child, I considered the United Nations my playground and my destiny. My father ran the UN Visitors' Service. This meant that he hired and supervised the "girl guides," as the tour guides then were known. Each morning he briefed them on global crises and conferences taking place at UN headquarters, and at the end of most days he schmoozed with other career bureaucrats and diplomats at cocktail receptions hosted by one foreign delegation or another. I've no idea how or when my parents first decided that the

UN was the ideal vacation environment for a seven-year-old. Perhaps my mother, a fan of *Eloise*, thought the Secretariat should stand in for the Plaza in her daughter's real-life edition. More likely she wanted Dad to pick up the child-rearing slack on school holidays when she was stretched thin. My mother, at the time, was building a small business importing hand-woven fabric from India, where we had lived a few years earlier. My father typically was gone from our home in suburban Connecticut from 7 a.m., when he left for the train station, until 7:30 p.m., when he returned just in time for dinner. He was not a playful or otherwise involved father, and I sincerely doubt that our daddy-and-me days at the UN were his idea. Whoever initiated these outings, however, I took to them like primer to canvas.

I can't recall my father uttering a word to me on the train into the city. We'd sit in the smoking car as he puffed on one Kent after another and inhaled the *New York Times*. I'd pick at stray threads in my tights, connect the dots in my activity books, and watch through the nicotine haze as the train rocked back and forth and a hundred male heads bobbed in unison. Those men swayed with an unmistakable sense of purpose. They wore the executive uniform of power. They were commuting to New York City, and I was along for the ride.

The fading gold constellations on the ceiling of Grand Central Station confirmed my awe of Manhattan. This was where the heavens unfurled and the dots that really mattered got connected. And the way my father marched, rapidly and directly, without a second's hesitation or distraction, made it clear that nowhere in the city mattered more than the UN. I had to trot to keep up with him across the four long blocks to the familiar geometric buildings where flags of the world snapped in the wind whipping off the East River.

As we passed through the delegates' entrance in the General Assembly Building, the guards greeted Dad, "Good morning, Mr. Liu." My father, however, was never a delegate. Also, his office was in the basement. Today, I find these two facts telling; I didn't as a child. Then, I thought my father ruled the UN, if not the entire world. Certainly he was too important to spend his day with me.

I would sit at the back of the guides' briefing room for Dad's morning capsule of current affairs. This was how I learned that the capital of the Philippines was then Quezon City and that the tiny South Pacific island of Nauru wanted its independence. What such factoids had to do with the UN escaped my young brain, but they did convince me that my father knew everything of significance in The World.

After the briefing, he'd assign one of the guides to look after me for the rest of the day, and he would retire to his windowless office to deal with more pressing business. My minders usually were family friends, recently graduated from college, who'd signed on as guides for a couple of years before getting married. This was the 1960s, and the UN guides were a step up from airline hostesses, but they were very much of the same ilk. Neither job qualified as a career, and both guides and stewardesses in those days had to be female, slender, and poised. Many in both groups also worked as fashion models. Yet there seemed to me something uniquely glamorous about the guides. Yolanda, the daughter of one of my father's friends from China, sometimes shed her official navy blue uniform (fashioned after the US stewardess prototype) for a magenta cheongsam (international attire optional for UN guides). And Twing, the daughter of old friends of my mother's from Wisconsin, had recently graduated from Wellesley and was engaged to marry a future diplomat. Yolanda and Twing both kindly pretended to be enchanted by the boss's daughter and, between tours, we'd play Crazy Eights, Go Fish, and Old

Maid. I had no sisters at home. I was neither popular nor comfortable among my girlfriends at school. But in the guides' lounge, I belonged.

That large, low-ceilinged rectangular room sported cinderblock walls, Naugahyde sofas, and fluorescent lighting. In the mirrored corner, Indian guides wound their slim hips in saffron and turquoise saris, Africans rebalanced patterned headdresses, Thais adjusted sarongs, and everyone applied makeup. The lounge coffee table was a shambles of newsprint in seven different languages, copies of *Vogue* and *Harper's Bazaar*, and bulletins from the press office upstairs. One thing my father made abundantly clear was that the guides were the UN's ambassadors to the general public, so they had to have the intelligence and education to explain both the workings of the organization and its vital importance on the world stage. They had to speak fluently in multiple tongues. And they had to model the international spirit of the UN's mandate for peace. That said, they also had to meet the same appearance standards as contestants in the Miss Universe Pageant, which my father and I watched together religiously every year.

The message to me came loud and clear: I should grow up to look gorgeous, know a lot, and act sophisticated. As a chubby little girl with dimples, I didn't see much I could do about my looks—that would come later. But UN tours gave me an ideal opportunity to practice knowing things. Each tour lasted about an hour and covered all three UN Council chambers and the General Assembly Building. I made a game of seeing how many tours I could pack into a single day. I think my record was eight.

By age nine I could tell you who was the secretary general, what the exposure of ductwork in the ceiling of ECOSOC was meant to symbolize, which Ghanaian leader had donated the giant kente cloth that hung in the hall outside the General

Assembly, and which countries—in addition to the permanent five (United States, China, Great Britain, USSR, France)—made up the Security Council. At day's end, as I trailed my father around whichever reception preceded our return tromp to Grand Central, suave middle-aged men would roar their approval at my recitations. It was a foregone conclusion, at least in my mind, that I would grow up to guide my own tours of the UN and then, most likely, go on to a career in the foreign service. Most assuredly I would marry a man who knew how to balance a highball and cocktail sausage and correctly pronounce *détente*.

My family's history supported this romantic forecast. My parents had met in Washington, DC, during WWII, when my father was a correspondent for the China News Service and my mother wrote for the women's section of the *Washington Star*. In her later years, Mom would say longingly, "We were so beautiful together." And they were. Dad was born of an American mother and Chinese father in Shanghai, where he picked up a dapper British accent and a fondness for Borsalino hats and single-breasted suits. My mother came from Scottish and German stock in Milwaukee, and in DC she fashioned herself into a cross between Audrey and Kate Hepburn. She lived for style the way Dad lived for news.

Our family's true nationality, according to my mother, was "international." In part, her label referred to our mix of heritage, but it had more to do with my father's career. He joined the UN shortly after its inception in 1945, working for refugee relief. His posting to the documentary film division gave us our two years in India. And he would spend more than a decade running the guided tour service. In truth, Dad was a career bureaucrat. Mom, however, insisted that she had married an "international diplomat."

The upshot for me was that, while the all-white girls in my

Connecticut elementary school wondered which of the boys next door they'd marry, I figured I'd have to circle the globe at least once before locating my future husband. They might raise their families in Riverside, Darien, or, if they married really well, back-country Greenwich, but the only home other than Manhattan that I could imagine for my adult self was Paris, London, or Tokyo.

The primer that seemed to have clung so naturally to my father's canvas began peeling before it was even dry. My UN visits ended when I was twelve, on one particular evening, in a single instant.

My parents and I had attended a UN Day celebration of world music in the General Assembly that evening. As was often the case at such galas, several notable celebrities were on hand. At the reception following the performance, a press photographer snapped me gazing up at Sidney Poitier.

I was too thrilled to be self-conscious. This dazzlingly debonair superstar who had broken down color barriers and won the Academy Award was one of my family's all-time heroes. The following day, however, when my father brought the printed photograph home from the office, Mr. Poitier receded into the background.

Forty years later that picture remains frozen in my mind. I look at least twenty. I wear a sleeveless red Jackie Kennedy sheath, which accentuates my precocious curves, and nylons and pumps that elevate my precocious height. My long dark hair flips up at my shoulders. Mr. Poitier smiles appreciatively, as he might at any attractive college girl. Looking on, my parents beam. This, their expressions telegraph, is their beautiful daughter, the one they raised to fit this exact image.

The trouble was, when I saw that photograph at twelve, I did not recognize myself. More to the point, the young woman in the picture mortified me. I had no idea how or why, but I knew she was a lie.

Over the following year, I intentionally shed forty pounds and all discernible curves. I gave away that red sheath, along with my John Meyer A-line skirts, Ladybug minis, and other confident coed fashions. I started dressing in baggy jeans and spending my spare time in the art room, where Miss B. let us spin Jimi Hendrix. When Hendrix wailed, "Are you experienced?" he wasn't talking about touring the United Nations. I was not experienced. Nor did I want to be.

I did, however, want to satisfy my parents' expectations. Or, rather, I could not imagine *not* satisfying them. The question was, how could I split the difference between the daughter they so happily had glimpsed impressing Sidney Poitier, and the clueless girl I knew myself to be? Trickier still, how could I figure out what it was about that photograph that felt so treacherous—and prevent it from defining my future?

For the next decade, I groped for an acceptable compromise. I developed anorexia but won my father's approval by joining the Wilhelmina Modeling Agency. (One of his former guides, a cover girl named Annabelle, schooled me on makeup and clothes for test shots.) Until the sample fashions began to swim on my shrinking figure, I earned enough from modeling to build my own college fund. My friends dropped acid and peddled hashish, but I earned straight As and went to Yale, and was too terrified of losing control to do any serious drugs. In college, I took no classes on foreign policy or international relations, but I did study painting, which had been my mother's major. After graduation, I moved directly into Manhattan and, just as directly, quit painting. Instead of going to work at the United Nations, I waited tables at Peartree's, a tony restaurant directly across the street from UN Plaza. And while I never actually dated any diplomats, at a party above the restaurant one night I was accosted and nearly raped by an ambassador. *Does that count?* something inside me kept asking. *Will that qualify me for whatever it is I still have to prove? Is that enough?*

My father by this time had reached the UN's mandatory retirement age of sixty. His career over, he now spent his days at home. But given that the house and suburbs had always been my mother's domain, Dad was not particularly comfortable or popular at home. It doubtless would have given him great joy if I'd launched my career at this moment in the realm he considered his own. And yet he never said a word when, instead of applying for a job as girl guide, I became a flight attendant for United.

My mother was as baffled by this choice as she'd been by my waiting tables. Surely there was some better use I could make of my Yale education. But before she had a chance to say this out loud, I sent her and my father off around the world. International travel passes were one of the perks of my new job.

Meanwhile, I began writing to try to make sense of the lie that continued to haunt me. My first book was a memoir that helped me connect a few dots and distance myself from my eating disorder. However, at twenty-four I was still working far too close to the page to see the big picture.

As predicted, I circled the globe and found my husband. But he was hardly what I'd expected. Not a diplomat, or even a bureaucrat, and certainly no member of the foreign service, Marty was a Jewish Bronx-born movie producer. He preferred hot dogs to cocktail sausages and eschewed highballs, did his balancing on the basketball court, and to my knowledge had never uttered the word *détente*. But he possessed a qualification that I hadn't even known I craved: he made me laugh.

Marty's group had come from Hollywood to China to scout film locations at the same time my parents and I were visiting my father's birthplace with a UN tour group. Our paths crossed on the Great Wall in May of 1979. Five months later, I moved from New York to Los Angeles.

Four years after that, we were married in Manhattan. As a gesture of respect for my parents, who were still struggling to come to terms with their daughter's erratic trajectory, our wedding took place at the ecumenical Church Centre for the United Nations.

Though I'd recovered my physical health by the time Marty met me, I had no job and less than a month's rent in the bank. I'd quit flying to "become a writer," but my memoir's publication was followed in short order by an attempt at a novel that my agent instructed me to burn. My professional identity seemed to be spinning backwards. My dowry, when I arrived in LA, consisted of a carton of melamine plates.

Yet, secretly, I still believed that the woman I was supposed to become wore designer business suits, carried an attaché case, and could toss off policy statements, treatises on global initiatives, and in-depth field reports on third world countries as if they were small talk. She excelled at cocktail parties, for which she maintained an assortment of little black Audrey Hepburn dresses, preferably from Bendel's or Bergdorf's. And even if she didn't reside in Manhattan, she'd spend enough time there to justify a pied-à-terre. This fully realized grown-up really would be able to banter with the likes of Sidney Poitier.

For another ten years I tried on jobs like personae, searching for one that might yet evolve into that old future self. Since writing came naturally to me, I tried editing magazines and trade papers, then shifted into cable and TV news production. But my beats were psychology and health, never global affairs. The disconnect persisted between *what* I was doing and *who* I was supposed to become.

"Oh, you should be," people often will tell friends wrestling with career choices, "an artist!" Or a model, a journalist, or a flight attendant. Usually, these are just helpful suggestions, gestures toward a direction the friend might or might not consider. But ever since my teens I'd lunged at these cues as if they came from on high. So when a colleague at NBC said, "You should go on air," it never occurred to me to doubt him.

I could become a broadcast correspondent. Sure I could. My father had launched his career by working as a foreign correspondent. Maybe *this* was the compromise I'd been searching for?

To start, I needed a demo reel. This did not pose a major obstacle. I was then producing health segments for the *Today* show. For my reel, I'd simply take some of the scripts I wrote for Dr. Art Ulene, read them myself on camera, and edit the stand-ups together. Our camera crews were friendly and willing. I'd spent years modeling. This should be a breeze.

Instead, when I faced the lens, every muscle in my body rebelled. My cheeks twitched. My neck froze. My voice cracked as erratically as the San Andreas Fault. I yanked my face into a smile and fought to deliver my lines, but the words wadded like Kleenex on my tongue.

My adolescent self might have been able to con the camera fifteen years earlier, but now the lens worked me like a lie detector test. *Do you know why you're doing this? Do you really want your face and voice blasted into the homes of strangers every night? Do you have even the slightest genuine interest in the life you're auditioning for?*

No, I thought. No, and no.

As it had when I was twelve, the camera trapped an image that rang an internal alarm. But this time the image was not polished, precocious, and fake. This image shook with truth.

When the producer who had encouraged me to go on-air saw my demo, he asked, "What happened?"

What happened, I realized, was that my body had declared what my mind didn't dare to: I had to stop chasing myself through other people's eyes.

Shortly after making that disastrous demo reel, I quit television and began to write books, not as a capital-A Author but as a small-c coauthor, writing down the wisdom of medical and scientific experts whose names appeared first on the book jackets. It finally had dawned on me that the important thing was not to "be a writer" (any more than it was to "be" a model, flight attendant, anchorwoman, or diplomat), but to write and, through writing, to discover what I most needed to learn.

Two books about babies and infant development preceded the birth of my son; three books about general psychology helped me make sense of my family, marriage, and friendships. A celebrity business book, which I ghostwrote, offered me a glimpse into a world of mansions and private jets that once might have enticed me; now, I viewed it as Mars.

Coauthorship served as a kind of apprenticeship. It gave me practice stitching words together into coherent sentences, chapters, and stories. Those years proved I could go the distance, writing one book-length manuscript after another. Best of all, I didn't have to put on a business suit and heels, face a camera, or schmooze at receptions as part of my job. Even if I wasn't always a ghost, I was largely invisible, and that suited me just fine.

Because the books I coauthored were mostly self-help and reference guides, words like *United Nations*, *foreign service*, and *international* didn't get much play in them, but the global strands running through my heritage were still profoundly present, if quiet. Like strings in a piano, they would always be part of me. I could choose to ignore them and perform safely in a higher octave, but a smarter, richer choice would be to incorporate them into a new piece that worked the entire instrument of my identity. For me, that new piece was fiction.

In 1989, as NPR captured the sound of gunfire and tanks rolling over pro-democracy demonstrators in Beijing's Tiananmen Square, I felt as if I were listening to an echo of my own family history: my father's father had been a pro-democracy activist against the Manchu dynasty that ruled China in 1900. Like the students in the square, he was a scholar revolutionary, a poet, calligrapher, protester, and strategist. After the Manchus were toppled in 1911, he became a politician and a true diplomat. He attempted to unite the warring factions of his fledgling government and to negotiate fair treaties for China with the Japanese, the Soviets, and Western powers. He married an American beauty with great style, and they raised four children through the Warlord Era, but his commitment to politics ultimately cost him his family. As WWII approached, my grandmother decided she'd had enough of the danger and uncertainty that came with her husband's chosen career, and she moved with her sons and daughters back to America. My handsome, distant, inscrutable father was their eldest son.

I had always known this history in a vague, preoccupied sort of way. But both these grandparents had died before I had a chance to know them, and before 1989 the gap between their ancient lives and my modern world seemed too immense to bridge. The events unfolding in Tiananmen Square told me that gap was vastly smaller than I'd realized. It consisted of a single generation, which my fingertips could span on a keyboard—in this case, the keyboard of my computer.

My family's story was more than a tale of star-crossed lovers; it was the source of questions that had pulsed beneath the surface of our "international" identity for as long as I could remember. What would motivate the union of a man and woman from backgrounds as different as nineteenth-century China and America? What possibilities did such a union represent? What were the consequences of its failure? How did this legacy play out in the lives, talk, and choices of such a couple's descendants?

The truth I'd never dared mention to my parents was that, when visiting the General Assembly as a child, I used to doze off as the simultaneous interpreter's voice droned in my earpiece. When scanning the memoranda on my father's desk, I couldn't fathom how anyone could penetrate international bureaucratese. I might have memorized the tours and enjoyed the building's important atmosphere, but my early exposure to the UN had left me with a secret dread of the actual work that was done there. The story of my family, however, offered a *living* version of international relations, and when I delved into it as a novelist, I found it anything but dull.

For the first time in our lives, my father and I spent hours talking as I researched his history. He told me about the night in 1916 when his mother came down with diphtheria while escaping from a death threat against his father in Peking. He recalled the racist bullying he endured from his British classmates in Shanghai. He showed me wartime letters from his father scrawled in English with a calligrapher's brush. In 1939, my grandfather had written from Chungking to his estranged wife in America, "My house in Hankow was burned by government order before they leaved there. Then in Nanking, in Kuling, in Hankow, my property will be lost all. The condition in here will be passed quickly. I do not know how to do in future." My grandfather had been a refugee just a few years before my father began working in refugee relief.

These slips of history danced like notes in a melody that kept morphing into new variations. The more I learned, the more I needed to know. I began to view my parents not as the dominant figures in my life, but as characters in a story that encompassed us all. My job was to write that story as completely and as truthfully as I possibly could.

One novel based on my international heritage multiplied into two, then three. A few months ago, I began work on a fourth. Each new story unfolds the past in a way that opens my future.

My father died last year at ninety-five, in my childhood home in Connecticut, with my mother and me by his side. We had made our final trip to the UN a decade earlier. By then, Dad had been retired for twenty-five years, but the way he strutted and beamed as we passed those familiar snapping flags and entered the lobby beneath Foucault's Pendulum made it clear that this was still where he felt he belonged.

As we approached the public information desk, it became just as clear that my father's legacy had evolved. Waiting to lead us on the tour that Dad himself had created was a guide he never would have conceived of hiring: a young man. My father looked at me with a wistful grin and lifted both palms in that universal gesture that asks, *What are you going to do?*

AIMEE LIU is the author of three novels—*Flash House, Cloud Mountain,* and *Face*—and two memoirs—*Gaining: The Truth about Life after Eating Disorders* and *Solitaire.* She has contributed to several anthologies, including *For Keeps, My California,* and *I'm on My Way Running.* Her articles, stories, and book reviews have appeared in many publications, including the *Los Angeles Times* and *Poets & Writers.* Ms. Liu was a recipient of the Association of Yale University Alumni Centennial Award of Honor, 2001. Her first novel, *Face,* was a Barnes & Noble Discover Great New Writers selection in 1994. She is a former president of PEN Center USA West and a member of the faculty of Goddard College's MFA program in creative writing. Her Web site is http://www.aimeeliu.net.

SOMEONE LIKE ME, BUT YOUNGER

Joyce Maynard

The man across the table from me was thirty years old, maybe, meaning that I was already married, with my first child on the way, around the time he got out of diapers. We had gotten together to discuss a project of mine that interested him, but as the meal progressed, he was expressing other interests.

I wasn't going to get involved with someone the age of my daughter, but I was definitely flattered by his attention. I could feel myself shifting slightly from the motherly role I'd adopted when we met, to something a little

31

different, and as dinner moved toward dessert, I could feel him looking at me less in the way a boy looks to his mom, and more the way a man looks at a woman. "I wasn't expecting you to be so hot" was how he put it. This was not a reference to menopause.

I confess, I enjoyed this. I had let my hair out of its clip. I fingered the pendant around my neck. I studied his unlined forehead and reflected on how long it had been since I'd faced a man across a table this way, who still had all his original hair, a man for whom career disappointments and knee injuries and crummy divorces had not yet clouded the horizon. A man who never gave a thought to his prostate gland. A man still young, in other words.

"You're really something," he said, when I came back from the ladies' room, where—it is true—I had checked my lipstick as I wouldn't have felt a need to do if it had been one of my sons with whom I was dining, instead of someone who probably listened to the same music and hung out at the same clubs. At hours when I am likely to be in bed. Alone.

"Thank you," I said, and I could look him in the eye here, where once I might have blushed or looked away. At the age of fifty-three—eighteen years since my divorce, with no shortage of relationships in my past, but having lived on my own now for longer than I lived with either parents or husband—I no longer assume as I once did that being unattached is a transitory condition for me. If there was a time when I viewed my single life as a period of waiting for the real life that would begin when the right man came along, that day is long gone. And with it has come a certain regret, for sure, but also an undeniable sense of strength and assurance. I have done okay without a partner for a long time now. I will continue to do so. Not that I wouldn't love to be in love with someone who loves me back, and (because this next does not automatically follow the first set of conditions) be able to put my life together with that of this other person. But I don't feel the same hunger I once did, to partner up before the ark sets sail.

I have gotten past the uncertainties I used to feel when someone gave a compliment. Time was, I stopped to consider what my strategy might be here. Now my rules are simple ones: Do what I want. Say what's on my mind. If the other person doesn't like that, it's better to find that out sooner rather than later.

"I mean it," he went on. "The girls I meet . . . the girls I go out with . . . they're playing all these games. It's so great to be around a woman who's not putting on some kind of act. Someone that's just totally real."

"It took a while," I said. "You have to do all that other stuff before you figure out that approach doesn't work."

"I wish . . ." he began.

I looked at him. He reached his hand across the table for mine.

"I wish I could find someone just like you," he said. "Only younger."

Someone like me, but younger. You might as well say someone who sings like Aretha Franklin, only white. George W. Bush, but smart.

"That person doesn't exist," I told him. "Even when I was young myself, I wasn't like me now."

Which brings me to the gift older women possess, that nobody can take from us; the one thing age (brutal as it may be) cannot wither, nor custom stale, because in fact, only age produces it. It is the ability to be ourselves, at last. After thirty, forty, or fifty years of worrying what everybody else thinks about us and trying to make people happy, an older woman knows at last that you can't please all the people all the time, or even most of the people most of the time. All you can do maybe is please yourself.

I doubt this state of being would appear so noteworthy to me if it hadn't been preceded by a few decades of a very different kind of behavior. Speaking for myself, but with the recognition that I am hardly alone in this, I will admit to having spent many long and frustrating years trying to transform myself into the person I needed to be, for my relationships with men to work. Not that this resulted in wonderfully successful relationships, mind you. (One is all it takes, actually.) But when they didn't work, it surely wasn't for lack of effort expended. Maybe just the opposite. Too much.

Never mind how this occurred, but the other night I tuned in to a reality show, which happens to be a sick addiction of mine: *The Bachelor*—a show in which a man the TV audience is meant to view as an undeniable catch as a husband is asked to select his future bride from a field of fifteen eager contestants. (We are further expected to take on faith the fundamental concept that a husband is what every reasonable young woman in America should want, and that any one of these fifteen would be happy to be chosen. The possibility that one of them might not want him is not a question anybody's asking here.)

This season's bachelor, Andy, like all the others who preceded him, was handsome in a toothpaste-commercial kind of way—a military doctor and triathlete, with the abs to prove it, who expressed a desire to find (over the course of ten episodes) his soul mate, life partner, mother of his children, and all-around companion on the jogging trail of life. The women, ranging from cute to knockout, ages twenty-three to twenty-eight, had been selected to move into a mansion in Santa Monica, where they would submit to a rigorous selection process (starting with an athletic competition, followed by a group date on a yacht), in which a few of them would be eliminated every week, culminating in the great moment when The Bachelor would choose his lucky bride.

Part of what struck me, watching this—invariably stupefied but unable to turn off the set—was the unquestioned assumption that these young women would want to be picked in the first place. But the bigger shock was their assumption that the way to Andy's heart lay in their success at putting on the best possible show for him—of athletic prowess, a positive attitude, bubbly personality (God forbid anyone on this show actually had a problem), commitment to home and family, and great cooking skills. The idea that any one of them might adopt the approach of "I'll just be myself and let the chips fall where they may" was about as alien to these young women as it would have been if one of them had allowed herself to show up for breakfast or her exercise workout without makeup.

Maybe a person has to live through a few failed relationships—or a few dozen failed relationships—to learn that, sooner or later, the truth about who you really are is likely to slip out. If being yourself isn't going to work with somebody, it's probably best to determine that fact before you head off on the Hawaiian honeymoon so many of the young women on *The Bachelor* seemed fixated on. ("Describe your dream wedding," one of them asked The Bachelor the other night—in a rare moment when the tables were turned, very slightly, toward checking out the man. But the question wasn't "What kind of marriage would you like?" or "What kind of relationship?" It had more to do with locale, size of guest list, color scheme.)

So I'm back to this question of who a woman would be if she were like me, but younger, as my dinner companion envisioned her. The younger part would involve a flatter stomach probably, fewer lines around my mouth and eyes, a look around my knees I can achieve now, for a moment, if I gather up the extra skin around that vicinity and pull it up a little as a person would who was smoothing a bedspread or putting on stockings. (An activity that dates a person, as precisely the kind of person who does need to pull up the extra skin around her knees, by the way. Because someone the age of my daughter, say—or the age of those young women on *The Bachelor*—has probably never pulled on a stocking of this sort or fastened a garter in her life.)

But as for what the "like me" part of this hypothetical ideal woman looks like—I think I know. It's the part that doesn't try to please anymore, or at least not the way a younger woman would. Who I am now is a woman in possession of the belief that the only way anyone's likely to be happy with me is if he knows who I am and decides that's fine by him. Sooner or later, I'll end up being myself anyway. I might work really hard at being the woman a certain man might find irresistible, to the point where he did find me irresistible. Only where would that get me? I'd have to keep up the act forever. So, never mind.

When I was young and I wanted a man to love me, I worked at it, and if things didn't turn out the way I wanted, I believed I'd failed. Now I figure whatever happens is what was supposed to take place. There is no such thing as letting some terrible revelation about myself slip out by accident, because whatever slips out is the truth of who I am, and if who I am doesn't suit a person, I'd better not be with him.

"We could have such a good time if you could just be nice," a man told me, not so long ago. A man I loved, with whom I had been very much hoping I might have a future. "If you would only . . . behave," he said. "Things could be wonderful."

For him, perhaps. But the truth was, the times I wasn't nice were also the times I was most myself. My moments of what he perceived as acting up were, in fact, my moments of greatest authenticity. After years of hiding those parts of myself away, in the interest of keeping the peace, I had come to the recognition that this kind of peace, these kinds of wonderful times, bore too high a price.

I love men, but I don't need one anymore, the way I did when I was young. (And I wanted someone to be a father for my children. And then, I wanted someone to raise them with me.) The ability to take care of my own self wasn't an aptitude I had sought out, but after many years of having to do that, I acquired it, and once acquired, it is not a skill that disappears. I couldn't conceal it now if I wanted to. This is either good news or bad, depending on the man. I'm not looking for him to be my world. I have one already. It is the biggest thing I acquired, over the course of all those years I was busy watching the gray hair move in and the lines take up residence in my forehead. I became my truest self, and though The Bachelor wouldn't hand me the coveted rose, signaling that I was in the running for the big prize, the good news is, I wouldn't choose him either.

JOYCE MAYNARD has been a reporter for the *New York Times*, a magazine journalist, radio commentator, and syndicated columnist, as well as the author of five novels, including *To Die For*, which became a successful film. Her best-selling memoir, *At Home in the World*, has been translated into nine languages. She appears regularly as a storyteller with The Moth in New York City and serves on the faculty of the Stonecoast Writing Program in Maine. Mother of three grown children, she makes her home in Mill Valley, California, and Lake Atitlan, Guatemala, where, in addition to pursuing her own work, she runs writing workshops. Her Web site is http://www.joycemaynard.com.

MOUTH OF WEBSTER, HEAD OF CLAY

Alan M. Dershowitz

We didn't have mirrors in my house, so I rarely got to look at myself when I was growing up. My grandmother had an old full-length mirror and, when I visited her, I would occasionally get a glimpse of what I looked like to others. What I saw was a skinny kid with curly red hair, full of energy, with a mischievous smile. I was not smart as a kid, but I was a smart aleck. I certainly wasn't wise, but I was a wise guy. My stock in trade was being funny, flirtatious, athletic, and a bane to the existence of all my teachers. I lived in a small, close-knit Orthodox Jewish community, and my mischievous reputation was well known. So when the time came to try to get a date for my senior prom, I decided to ask a pretty girl who didn't live in the neighborhood, in the hope that neither she nor her parents would be aware of my reputation. The problem was that the school—an Orthodox yeshiva—had established a three-member committee to which we had to apply for a prom date. What happened when I applied provides a fairly good summary of my status at that point in my life.

I will never forget the three teenage girls who sat in judgment of my dating request. They sat there like prima donnas, telling us who we could and could not ask to the prom. There was a long line. When my turn came, Barbara—the most arrogant of the three—demanded of me the name of the girl I wanted to ask. When I mentioned Karen's name, the three girls burst into uncontrollable laughter at my chutzpah. "Karen is on the A-list," Helene asserted. "You're on the C-list. You have to pick somebody from either the C- or the D-list," Gladys insisted, handing me a copy of the dreaded lists that contained the names of all the unpopular girls. I saw the name of one of my cousins on the list and decided to ask her. So, one loser took another loser to the prom. That was my life back then.

I did no better academically than socially. In yeshiva high school, I was placed in what was called the "garbage class," reserved for the worst discipline cases and taught by a disciplinarian who would have been more at home as the warden of a juvenile prison. We were not particularly good prisoners, but we did have a code of silence. When my friend Alan Bachman took my jockstrap out of my basketball gym bag and threw it at the teacher, I was blamed. The evidence was clear, since my mother put my name tape on everything I owned, even my jockstrap (as if someone else would want to wear it).

Res ipsa loquitur—the thing speaks for itself. Even though Bachman was the culprit, our code demanded that I not rat him out, and so I took the punishment like a man. But I had to get even with the teacher. It was wintertime, and in my locker I had a heavy coat, snow pants, boots, and a hat. I stuffed them with paper towels and created a dummy of myself. Working with an accomplice named Jake Greenfield, I took my dummy up to the roof of the building and aimed it right past the window where my teacher was holding class. Jake ran down to the teacher and screamed, "Dersh is jumping off the roof! He can't take being suspended. Quick, look out the window!" As the poor, beleaguered teacher looked out, my "body" hurtled past him to its imminent death. The teacher nearly had a heart attack, until he saw my "body" break apart into various pieces as it hit the pavement. Needless to say, I was suspended for a month and went to the Brooklyn Public Library, where I began to educate myself.

There were two areas in which I was extremely successful and one in which I was moderately successful, even in those bad old days. I was the best debater in school and I was popular with my fellow students, which led me to run for student body president. Because of my academic deficiencies, they took my name off the ballot, but I continued to run as a write-in and came within a few votes of defeating the establishment candidate. Having lost that election, I decided to establish an inter-yeshiva council, which did not require the permission of the principal. I ran for its presidency and won. Also, I was moderately successful at basketball, making the varsity team in my junior year as a bench player. I would have started in my senior year, but I was suspended for academic reasons. We played in

Madison Square Garden, where one of the opposing guards was a short, extremely well-dressed boy named Ralphie Lipchitz, now better known as Ralph Lauren.

As I was about to graduate, my principal called me in for a career talk. "You got a good mouth on you, but not a particularly good head. You should pick a career where you have to do a lot of talking, but not a lot of thinking. Maybe you should be a lawyer." (The principal was an Orthodox rabbi, and he also suggested that I might consider becoming a conservative rabbi, which to him was a grave insult.) The rabbi was not the only person who had negative views about my brain power. The original draft of my yearbook described me as having "a mouth of Webster and a head of Clay." My mother made them change it.

I applied to Columbia University and was rejected. I did not have high enough grades to get into Brooklyn College, which was free to New York residents but hard to get into. Fortunately, they had a test that they used in combination with grades, and I managed to get a high enough score to make it in by the skin of my teeth. Though a bad student in high school, I was always a good test taker and wanted to take the New York State Scholarship Exam—a highly competitive test that provided funding for education. Because I came from a family of very modest income, it was important for me to win the scholarship so I would not have to work part-time during college. My school forbade me to take it, setting up an arbitrary rule that only students with eighty averages or better could take the exam. They established this arbitrary rule so that the percentage of state scholarships won by the school would be artificially inflated. I filed a complaint with the New York Board of Education and prevailed. I took the exam and won the scholarship. To this day, the principal thinks I probably copied my answers, despite the fact that nobody else seated near me won the scholarship.

My mother was so worried about me while I was in high school that she took me for an occupational test at the New York State Department of Employment. The test results established that I would make a good advertising executive, salesman, or funeral director. My mother asked them, "Why not a lawyer?" They responded that a lawyer has to finish college and they weren't sure that I would get into any college or law school.

But I did get into college and everything changed. A few of my teachers told me that I was actually smart, that my problem was motivation rather than intelligence. Brooklyn College provided the motivation. I immediately became a straight-A student, which frightened my parents almost as much as my straight-Cs in high school had embarrassed them. "You should get Bs," my mother would always say. "If you get As, you'll become a teacher, and you won't make a good living, and if you get Cs, you'll end up selling shoes. Bs are good. You could become an accountant or maybe even a lawyer, especially with your big mouth."

I became president of the student body, captain of the debate team, and a star intramural athlete. By this time, I knew there were no limits on what I could do. I quickly learned, however, that there was one important limit: I was enthusiastically recommended by the college administration for a coveted Rhodes Scholarship to Oxford, but the elitist Rhodes Committee was not considering Jews from Brooklyn as appropriate candidates, and I wasn't even given an interview. That was the first time I realized that my background and religion could hold me back. That realization became a dramatic reality when, as a Yale Law School student, I was turned down by thirty-two Wall Street firms. Though I was first in my class, editor in chief of the law journal, and a future Supreme Court law clerk, those qualifications were trumped by my religion and ethnicity. Welcome to the real world of discrimination, circa 1960.

By the mid-1960s, that, too, had changed, with the advent of the civil rights movement and the passage of antidiscrimination laws. There were still some barriers, but they were not particularly relevant to the life path I had chosen. I wanted to become a teacher, a law professor. I was offered jobs at Harvard, Yale, Stanford, Columbia, Chicago, and all the other elite law schools. I was also offered jobs in government and at law firms. Suddenly, everybody seemed to want a Jewish kid from Brooklyn, with a big mouth and high grades.

Thinking back to my years in elementary and high school, I never could have imagined my future life as a law professor, lawyer, writer, and public intellectual. Nor could any of my friends or classmates. A funny story that took place a few years ago in California well summarizes the change. I was speaking to a large group of people in Los Angeles. After the talk, a man about my age came up to me and asked if I was related to Avi Dershowitz, whom he had known as a kid in Brooklyn. Unbeknownst to him, I am Avi Dershowitz—that was the Hebrew nickname by which I was known until I got into college and my parents persuaded me I needed a real name. I didn't tell him I was Avi and, instead, decided to play a joke on him. I said, "Yeah, I am related to Avi." He then asked me, "Whatever became of him?" I responded sadly, "He ended up badly." The man replied, "I knew he would come to no good."

ALAN M. DERSHOWITZ is the Felix Frankfurter Professor of Law at Harvard Law School and one of the United States' principal appellate lawyers. Known as a consistent defender of

First Amendment rights, he has earned a powerful voice in how the Constitution is interpreted. A regular contributor to the *New York Times*, he is the author of the *New York Times* best seller *Chutzpah*, as well as *The Vanishing American Jew*, *Why Terrorism Works*, *Shouting Fire*, *The Case for Israel*, *Reversal of Fortune*, and *Reasonable Doubts*.

CATHY BLAIVIS

MINDFULLY

Lee Chamberlin

Our temperaments are etched in our faces. Our inner life determines the cast of our eye, softens or hardens our jaw, and reveals our past and present states of mind. As a kid, I studied faces. As a woman, I continue to question the eyes of men, the mouths of women, and the postures of familiar and unfamiliar faces by which human strengths and frailties display themselves when shrouded in silence.

In the summer of 1999, a comprehensive Rembrandt exhibit at London's National Gallery included the seventeenth-century Dutch master's series of self-portraits, a forty-year chronicle of his altering physical appearance. His objective detachment of subject from artist is frank, unforgiving, and, at times, ruthless. I wondered, Are these soul-baring self-assessments an opportunity to narrate his life as he wanted it disclosed? Are these painted chapters a guarantee of immortality, or an invitation to us to speculate about the outward effects of his inner consciousness and the way in which he lived? Did he intend to lay bare personal inventory of unsympathetic and unsuspected inner truths, or are these masterworks an art lesson in portraiture on various textures of wood, cloth, and smooth-surfaced panels? Assuming none of this conjecture approaches the artist's true purpose, it can still be noted that the final outcome in no way lends itself to consider that Rembrandt indulged in the seventeenth-century equivalent of photographic retouching.

Rembrandt initially introduces himself as an unassuming young man of twenty-two, dressed in a simple, somber-colored jacket with no collar. His gaze is open and direct, free of any hint that he is much sought after, despite his youth, as a naturally accomplished artist who enjoys a substantial reputation as a teacher. His studio, filled with would-be acolytes, includes a well-known painter of the time a good deal older than his fresh-faced instructor. Rembrandt's marriage to the daughter of a successful art dealer puts him in contact with well-heeled patrons who commission his services. By the time he's thirty-three, he owns a magnificent townhouse in Amsterdam. His increased wealth and self-assurance are evident in an oil-on-wood in which he wears a fashionable flat-crowned, wide-brimmed hat and a dark-colored coat of extravagantly rich fabric he did not buy off the back of a pushcart. With greater success come portraits in which dual gold chains drape his neck; exotic helmets, plumed hats, and rakish berets crown his head. His hair is worn longer and combed in a more mature style. Squared shoulders declare unabashed, unapologetic material well-being. The pockmarked cheek and ruddier complexion of his late twenties confirm an artistic integrity that openly admits to less-flattering physical flaws.

By the time Rembrandt reaches his midfifties, his highly acquisitive living leads to a declaration of bankruptcy. The financial demands of his townhouse's upkeep eventually force him to move. Despite a decline in fortune and the pain in earlier years the death of his young wife and, by the end of his life, the death all of his four children surely brings, Rembrandt continues to scrutinize the inescapable evidence of his own mortality. It's all there, challenging us to equal probity as he acknowledges with candor and precision the progression of his physical metamorphosis.

A very bright six-year-old I know recently drew me a series of stick figures depicting his future career choices: a race car driver, a firefighter, and "When I finish being a firefighter," he declared, "then I'll be a policeman." Nothing seemed to stand in his way of becoming every figure he confidently drew. What's curious about my young friend's choices is none reflect the pleasure he gets from slipping away from the hubbub of his family's living room activities to seek sanctuary in his bedroom, stretched out on the floor with a book. His love of reading is obvious, yet no stick figure of "writer" made its way into his career gallery. Besides, what does a writer look like?

I don't recall growing up wanting to be anything specific. As a child, I was drawn to the arts and I read a good deal. I do remember announcing to my mother that once the Russians won the cold war, invaded America, and took over everything, I'd be spared their barbarism because I'd be considered an artist. My mother reacted with the sort of tolerant expression reserved for the harmlessly insane. Despite being designated "the leader" by friends I played with on my city block, I felt apart, removed from their interests and concerns, content to spend time alone. As soon as I was old enough, I liked nothing better than to go downtown, always alone, to lose myself in playwrights' stories that unfolded on Broadway and off-Broadway stages.

Hidden clues to our true natures manifest as impulsive, irrational, or compulsive acts. Unknowns about our authentic selves spring from innate predispositions. Who we are and what we see in the mirror are not only who we consciously create, but also who we allow to emerge. At seventeen, I entered a playwrights' competition for high school students sponsored by the American Cancer Society. I won first prize, a writing course at New York University, where I was enrolled as a freshman for that fall.

There are no writers, actors, or singers in my family, although my aunt, my mother's sister, who couldn't read a note of music and never had a music lesson in her life, could hear any tune once then sit down at a piano and play the hell out of the tune and the piano.

I am a playwright who took the long way around. I began my journey as an actress on New York City's off-off-Broadway musical stage. I worked up to a lead role in an off-Broadway musical, then auditioned my way into television as one of the six original cast members of *The Electric Company*, a Public Broadcasting Network program in variety-show format of comedic skits and song-and-dance routines to teach reading skills to youngsters. *The Electric Company* was, and remains to this day, the best and most cherished time of my life as an actress. It is also where I met Bill Cosby, our most prominent cast member, best known for his affinity for kids.

Before meeting Bill, I landed a small role in my first major motion picture, which I consider my second major motion picture, since most of what I filmed in the first one ended on the editing room floor, leaving an already small role looking more like a walk-on. It was the same year that Cosby recommended me for what I consider to be my truly first major motion picture, opposite him and Sidney Poitier. Sizable portions of my role ended on the cutting room floor as well, but with an important difference. Mr. Poitier, the film's producer, director, and star, took the time to apologize and patiently explain to me, a fledgling, box office realities about comedies. In order for them to be funny and profitable, they can't become audience endurance tests, as this one was threatening to do (shy the needed cuts). Happily, most of what I filmed survived the final editing process. On my last day of shooting, I was invited by Mr. P. to join the cast of his next movie, a totally unexpected invitation I eagerly accepted.

In the previous summer of 1973, in Joseph Papp's Shakespeare in the Park at the Delacorte Theatre in New York City's Central Park, I played Cordelia to James Earl Jones's King Lear. Five years into my seemingly chosen field brought me prominent roles in two stage musicals, guest artist and title role status at Penn State University in the Greek tragedy *Medea*, a Shakespeare with, in addition to James Earl Jones, acting bigwigs Raul Julia, René Auberjonois, Paul Sorvino, Ellen Holly, and Rosalind Cash, all of us directed by Broadway director Ed Sherin. No doubt about it, I was on a roll. If nothing else happened to me, I could look back on a short, lively, and fulsome experience that included a successful comedic television series, two big Hollywood movies, and a third film in the offing. An ambitious young woman, full of expectation and hope, but with no real career plan, was realizing a legitimate acting career. I couldn't have done better if I'd had a plan.

During a more socially restricted era in America, many women took up careers in teaching, tending the sick as nurses, or caring for their own families as housewives. Some women broke society's constraints and many of them made history in the process. In the severely racially restricted time and place of my mother's early life, status and position for women of color were more vigorously proscribed. As a consequence, she believed, as her mother had before her, that the primary duty of nonwhite women was to be perceived, and ultimately considered, *respectable*. As she looked to my future, my mother's vision reflexively contracted to a nursing career as my best and safest hope for respectability. Her career choice for me revealed how well she understood that respectability was considered a virtue unnatural to my race and gender. My status as an upright citizen of unimpeachable moral standards who contributes to the betterment of the community and the country was believed by most of white America to be impossible in principle, generally improbable in practice, and more often than not, in reality, highly implausible. These were things about America's less-enlightened aspects that my mother had learned from experience. These were harsh and difficult truths she kept from me. However, she never failed to mention, with shimmering pride, that she was a high school graduate, a boast and an accomplishment not many of her time and race could take for granted. On the occasions on which she trumpeted that accomplishment, she did so with the triumphant flair of having faced down nearly impossible odds.

In deference to my mother, I entered college as a pre-nursing student. With my bachelor's degree, I could teach nursing if I chose not to practice. I'd been an "A" student in chemistry and in most other subjects in high school. Nevertheless, in one short week, college chemistry covered in full what it had taken an entire year to study and master in high school. After the first week of college-level science, I was lost. My Dad used to tell me that there was nothing I couldn't do. I believed him, but here was a clear case that did not fit his maxim. I switched my major to French Literature and Language and my minor to English Lit. Because of my love for theater, I joined the campus theater club.

The Philadelphia Story is a tale of a wealthy upper-crust white family and their headstrong, rebellious daughter. Our theater club's mentoring professor made a point of apologizing for casting me as the maid in the piece, but I refused to see a problem. It was a part in a play and, like all the other cast members, I was simply playing a part.

In the following production, a three-act of dubious merit whose title escapes me, I was cast as an Egyptian belly dancer. I wore a gauzy costume with lots of veils on my face and sheer balloon pants covering my long, light brown legs. I was told I looked nice. My dialogue during all three acts consisted of as many lines spoken in a language I was asked to invent. This language was then "translated" by the only one of the play's characters who could understand me. In the scenes where I appeared without benefit of dialogue, and there were many such scenes, I entered, stood stock-still, looked straight ahead, then made my exit trailing the actor whose plot line I was connected to in some now long-forgotten way. These silent entrances, exits, and frozen poses were meant to be funny, except no one ever laughed. Call it bad staging, worse acting, or simply a lousy part. With the obvious metaphor inherent in that pointless character, I began to suspect the outside world held a different view of me than the one my father and I held. In subsequent play selections, our well-meaning prof could find no roles for me so he asked me to stage manage. Why not? I was nineteen. The world was still mine and nontraditional casting had yet to be invented.

When I was an undergrad at NYU's Washington Square College, Madame Germaine Brée chaired the French department. To my shiny, late-teenaged eyes, Madame Brée glistened like the first star of evening. Her wardrobe of expensive, well-tailored, classically designed knit dresses in varying shades of gray complemented her strong, attractive features, always makeup free, except for a subtle wisp of lip color. Every strand of her short, raven, expertly cut hair fell into place with a casual sweep of her nail-polish-free hand. When I learned she'd served in the French resistance during World War Two and had been friends with Albert Camus, my literary and philosophical hero of the moment, she embodied everything I ever wanted to be: scholarly, courageous, and a snappy dresser.

In the waning days of my sophomore year, I was invited to lunch at her apartment to discuss my impending fall trip to study in Paris, a trip my mother had suggested and for which my Dad was more than willing to pay. Two walls of Madame Brée's spacious Riverside Drive apartment's living room were lined, floor to high ceiling, with books. Natural light flooded past the bank of unadorned windows that faced Riverside Park and spilled onto the cream-colored bookcases. It was the perfect setting for the only college professor who demonstrated a genuine interest in me and in my future. (I don't count the professor notorious for his attempted and frequently successful seductions of unsuspecting coeds, who invited me to join his honors program. I declined on the grounds that I had never studied the subject on which he was such an expert, but he assured me he'd teach me all I needed to know to succeed in his class.)

Madame Brée's legitimate interest extended to coming to my defense against another professor, whose narrow, commonplace agenda my mother knew firsthand, growing up in a racially segregated New Jersey seaside town. As the department chair—the second woman in the college's history to head a department—Madame Brée was equally familiar with her second-in-rank's circumscribed points of view on race and women. A white professor, he questioned the validity of the degree I received from that venerable French institution of higher learning, L'Université de Paris. For no reason I could understand at the time, he challenged my year at the Sorbonne, as well as my overall academic record. In spite of my more than passing grades, he tried to deny me full college credit for my studies abroad. With customary dignity and absolute authority, Madame Brée overruled him, ensured that I received full academic credit for my studies in France, then invited me to join the French honors program she'd recently established for college seniors. Honors would be determined first by the level of each student's contribution to the seminar's weekly discussions conducted in French, second, by passing a stiff, year-end exam, and, finally, by submitting an A-worthy paper. I made honors, the only one of the eight candidates to do so. The only woman to do so. The only nonwhite candidate to do so. I wasn't the nurse my mother had hoped for, but she was proud of the respectability I achieved by graduating with honors in French, and doubly proud to add to her own educational boast a daughter who was now a college graduate.

I needed a job, but had no idea what I wanted to do in life. At the time, a bachelor's degree was the New York City Department of Welfare's only job requirement. I soon discovered that as a Welfare Department's version of a social worker, it was my duty to ask potential clients probing questions to get to the truth about their difficult situations. Based on my investigations of the claims of permanently disabled, blind, indigent, old, temporarily unemployed, and women with dependent children who streamed through the department's doors for help, my judgments and decisions determined the financial and related assistance I was authorized to give. I tried to resist the cynicism of some of the older hands on the job, but I admit to being occasionally duped by welfare applicants who knew how to work the system better than I knew how to spot their well-practiced survival skills. My decisions as the "Welfare Lady" altered lives. With only summer job experience to call on and with very little life experience, Welfare Department duties were too much to handle. After ten months, I quit.

My mother was a Baptist whose religious commitment consisted of wearing a new hat to show off at church service on Easter Sunday. Regardless of her slim link to Protestant practice, my mother took noisy issue with my lapsed Catholic father's decision to baptize me Catholic. In a rare display of religiosity, my Dad pointed out that unless the sins I'd committed during my five and a half years on earth were expunged in purgatory's fire, allowing heaven to eventually accept my burnished, purified spirit, I'd end up in limbo, a place for the undecided soul, heaven's waiting room, where I'd face perpetual, final destination uncertainty. I can only imagine the same tolerant expression my mother, reserved for the clearly demented who pose no physical danger to themselves or others, patiently conferred on my Dad. Dad's inflexibility on the baptism question, however, was most likely due to the neighborhood's physical wreck of a public school, a known dumping ground for the so-called uneducable, code for non-white students from poor families. That public school was no place for the academic goals my folks had in mind for me, especially since a Catholic school was literally next door to our apartment building.

At Our Lady of Lourdes Elementary, I metamorphosed into a religious, inquisitive, and studious kid, the kind who just loves to do homework. In those days, Catholic education taught logic and reason as points of pride. I developed questions about Catholic dogma that logic, reason, and the teaching nuns were unable or unwilling to answer. I was sent to "have a talk" with one of the parish priests for daring to have questions, and was cautioned by him that not accepting the tenets of the church on faith alone would cause me to lose my soul to everlasting damnation. Wow! Despite and maybe because such threats came from a man regularly seen weaving his way back to the priests' rectory from the local saloon four blocks away, I rejected every religious and dogmatic claim I'd ever been taught. My curiosity about God's intent and the nature of existence shrank along with my religious fervor. Dogmatic religion and God were no longer relevant to my life. In the neighborhood, word circulated that the stumbling, alcoholic parish priest had been hustled into rehab.

In the secular West, where the material outweighs all else, we are encouraged to trust only that which we can see and touch. Explanations of the intangible, when trapped in inflexible "truths," undercut what is possible to know of life and of ourselves through less accepted methods of enlightenment. What's deemed "impossible" dismisses faith in infinity and restricts to the physical senses the only means of apprehending a larger world.

Blaise Pascal, a French seventeenth-century whiz kid, mathematician, and physical scientist, faced doubts about God's existence and the nature of man's purpose. A near fatal accident left the mathematical theorist-philosopher unconscious for two weeks. Once revived, he jotted down notes of the "religious" vision he experienced during his coma and carried these notes with him at all times. In his treatise on Christian apologia, published posthumously as *Penseés*, Pascal dismisses reason as an uncertain route to the unknowable. In his essay "The Wager," he writes that since God's existence cannot be determined through reason, a person should bet and act as if God does exist, since it's a win if it's true and no loss if it isn't. When I read this essay in college, it jogged my occasional thoughts about the nature of existence in this artfully complex world and how this God fits into the overall equation, but I gave no real attention to the matter.

A strip of amusement arcades from roughly West Forty-second to West Fifty-fourth streets once dotted Broadway, New York's longest and busiest thoroughfare. In these mini amusement parks, four sepia-toned, two-by-two photographs could be yours for a quarter. For a dime, you could sing into a microphone in a telephone-booth-sized "recording studio" and get a shiny, black, 45-rpm vinyl record for your effort. I enjoyed making ten-cent amateur disks and soon owned a sizable collection of the cheap vinyls to prove it.

Soon after college, and encouraged by my new husband, I began professional voice training. I auditioned at local niteries for singing gigs, was eventually hired by the Playboy circuit and sent out of town to perform in every one of their venues across the country and in Montreal. In the insular world of club owners and music promoters, I earned a reputation as a "girl singer" who brought in business. Two-week stands on the road without friends or family is lonely stuff, but still more fun and far better paid than the Welfare Department. No Playboy bunnies in the Welfare Office to show me the *bunny dip*, a skill that requires a straight back, knees held tightly together in a modified, sideways plié, a tilt of the upper body toward the customer's table while balancing a full tray of drinks and heavy dinner plates on one shoulder and serving with the free hand. I never got the hang of the bunny dip. Fortunately, the hired entertainment never had to stand in for the bunnies.

Thanks to my husband's job with an international film company, we moved to Paris, where his business contacts opened doors I'd never have been able to pry open on my own. Paris's most influential talent agent's dynasty of entertainment impresarios was soon working on my behalf. A recording contract I signed with my agent's nephew included a music deal with still another nephew, whose publishing house provided songs for me to record and perform on stage. The French I'd honed as a student in Paris, in tandem with local show-biz nepotism, transformed me into a French chanteuse. After fifteen wonderful months that included an appearance at Paris's Olympia Theatre (the bygone, Sinatra-era equivalent of "playing the Palace"), and touring France in music festivals with the very best musicians, the clock struck midnight. My husband's Paris job ended. Our little family of three returned to New York, where our young daughter soon welcomed a baby brother. I abandoned singing, with its built-in out-of-town engagements, in order to study acting. Thus began thirty-six years as a working actress with remarkably little downtime. I actually made a living as an actress.

Material well-being is incapable of completing a life. As my marriage lurched to its predictable, materialistic dead end, I searched for ways to understand and remedy menstrual cycles of unusual duration, unnaturally heavy flow, and crippling pain. I learned that in metaphysics, blood represents life. The very life was flooding out of me. By surgically correcting the problem in what should have been a routine outpatient procedure, severe blood loss left me too weak to leave the hospital, and I was obliged to stay overnight. The next morning, my Dad took me to his place. When my husband came to my father's and asked if I was ready to go home, a column of air leapt upward along the center of my body in a propulsion of "energy" that settled in my throat and robbed me of all physical control over speech. An inner awakening assumed decisive autonomy. A calm, measured voice spoke in my stead. I listened and followed its advice when it repeated, "I'm not going back."

To be good at living, we must put ourselves on the line honestly and openly. No shortcuts. No sleight-of-hand. After leaving my marriage, I had near-nightly dreams of dirt being shoveled onto my face, suffocating me and burying me alive. Dream paralysis would block my throat and muffle my struggling, futile cries for help. Trails of light of inherent promise led me out of dream darkness, then faded and plunged me back into dream obscurity. The unanswered childhood questions that rendered God and dogmatic religion irrelevant soon returned as I wrestled with a way to live a fuller, more peaceful life. A wise man once proclaimed, "When the student is ready, the teacher appears." I believe I was ready to meet the teacher.

I have been charged to take an honest look at the face I see in the mirror and determine if it reflects the life I wanted or thought I'd lead. This is a task writers perform more or less knowingly as we cherry-pick our experiences, reshape and disguise them, before they are woven through our fictional stories.

Over the years, steady acting work in nighttime television supported my secret writing habit, a habit that turned into an openly practiced obsession.

My name as an actress never rose to the heights of household word. However, as a steadily working thespian, I was able to take proper care of myself throughout and to ante up the divorce-decreed financial contribution to my children's care, feeding, and educations. My "actor" face is occasionally recognized, even when the unfamiliar context of airport security line or supermarket aisle baffles and prompts the inquirer to ask, "Didn't you used to teach school in Brooklyn?" or "Didn't I meet you last year at a party at my cousin's?" After many acting seasons, nine years on a daytime soap opera provided the financial freedom to shape and shop my first stage play, until it found a home and a bit of success.

Not unlike my mother, I faced irrational, unenlightened odds as an actress, many of which remain stubbornly in place in my life as playwright. That said, I enjoyed acting challenges. I viewed not getting a part as something that, in the larger order, simply wasn't meant to be. Trust in the inevitability of such an order sustains a balance in my personal and larger worlds and allows me to accept life as it unfolds in its puzzling way and in its own good time. This creates a faith in life's inherent viability, until all problems appear to solve themselves. Life does possess natural cycles. Worry provides little of note, other than an occasion for hand-wringing over drinks with friends. I don't believe there is any such thing as chance. The chaos in which the world appears to find itself comes from man's determination to direct and control both method and outcome of personal agendas.

Through a near lifetime of searching, I discovered that how and what we think summon the vital energies that guide our lives and render all things possible. I use centuries-old methods of meditation, contemplation, and positive outlook to better realize what is possible in my life. I don't want to shortchange myself or those around me. I've learned to test blind faith in order to develop informed faith. I test my courage in order to live more honestly. All such effort notwithstanding, I remain deeply flawed.

Perhaps maturity accounts for the philosophy by which I have lived these last twenty years. By assessing life's unpredictability and coming to terms with the futility of fighting what I cannot control, I approach life in the way that Buddhists call *living mindfully*. I am not a Buddhist, but the face I see has been created by similar thoughts and related actions. I use the senses as a gateway to a calmer existence. I see, feel, hear, taste, and touch the physical moments and become immersed in acute awareness of self and of my surroundings. Out of that consciousness comes the realization that little is important, while all is important. The need and the impulse to fast-forward are suspended.

Since the tranquility that comes from living one moment at a time is daily challenged, there's nothing for it except to keep at it until the stage lights come down, the house lights come up, and the audience files out.

Plays can be classified as nearly perpetual works in progress. They are written, rewritten, read aloud in living rooms by friends who willingly give time and talent to the development process before the play is workshopped, rewritten yet again, and sent out to theaters wrapped in fragile hopes. The face I see in the mirror is also a work in progress. Nothing for it but to keep at it until the stage manager places a bare-bulbed, metal-shafted floor lamp near the lip of the stage. This theater work light's singular glare is a beacon and a reminder that although one play's run ends, another will surely take its place. Acting, singing, composing music, and writing lyrics and plays have combined to forge me into the person I have always been, a work in progress. Some of my friends say a dreamer, but what do they know of my hidden, inner life?

LEE CHAMBERLIN is a writer who also has enjoyed a successful career as a stage, film, and television actress. Her early stage work includes playing Cordelia to James Earl Jones's King Lear in the Delacorte Theatre's Shakespeare in the Park production. Lee won a Grammy for her participation in *The Electric Company* recording and was nominated for an Emmy as guest star on *Lou Grant*. Lee played opposite Sidney Poitier and Bill Cosby in the films *Uptown Saturday Night* and *Let's Do It Again*. An accomplished playwright and musician, she wrote the book, music, and lyrics for the award-winning 1988 musical *Struttin'*, which she also directed and opened off-Broadway to great acclaim. Her one-woman play, *Objects in the Mirror . . . (are closer than they seem)*, is a solo piece in which Chamberlin performs the roles of seven characters dealing with the indifference with which the world treats its dead. The play debuts in February 2010 at the Kitchen Theatre, Ithaca, New York.

I AM NOT MYSELF
AT ALL

Malachy McCourt

One of the boasts made by the righteous is "I work hard and I pay my taxes," which causes me to either laugh or suppress the urge to vomit. Most of the imbeciles who make this boast of their virtue are not aware that, according to their Bible, work is a punishment visited on Adam for eating an apple or Eve or both. Consequently, I, being aware that I did not commit whatever Adam & Eve are reputed to have committed, (A) do not accept the concept of original sin and (B) have carefully avoided or evaded work and any form of taxation where possible.

I was raised—or as was said in the holy city of Limerick, Ireland, I was dragged up—in that dreary town. Death, disease & despair were the order of the day, and most of the women were worn out bearing too many children, rearing those who lived, and mourning the third who died. The men were mostly out of work—or idle, as it was put—except for the few who were lucky enough to have the laboring jobs, manual labor being what we expected to be doing for the rest of our working lives and heaven help the kid who evinced an ambition to get a job indoors in a grocery shop or in an office as a clerk, or clark, as it was pronounced there. We were also victims of class distinctions, a relict of eight hundred years of British occupation, giving truth to Æ's (George Russell) observation that you eventually become the thing you hate most. So Ireland became a place of tuppence ha'penny looking down on tuppence.

One thing I was absolutely certain about in my Irish childhood was what I did not want to be, and that was me I myself. I hated the dirt, the smells of the buckets of shit and piss our neighbors emptied in the lavatory outside our door. I hated the lice in my hair and the millions of fleas feasting on my body and the general stink of poverty in the lane. I had to walk sideways on the street like a crab so that anyone walking behind me could not see my arse was out through my trousers. Then shame of shame, having to put black soot from the chimney on my ankle in a ridiculous effort to cover the holes in the back of my socks as we went up to the altar rail and knelt to receive the body of Jesus in full view of a judgmental jury of snobs posing as Christians. I was rejected for the job of altar boy due to the suspicion that all slum kids were too dirty to get near Christ, plus the fact they wore dirty clothes.

In response to "What are you going to be when you grow up?" it was always judicious to say you had a towering ambition to take Holy Orders if God so willed, or else there was a possibility of getting a job when you were fifteen sweeping horseshit off the streets of Limerick, of which there was no shortage at that time (horseshit, I mean). A good job, 'twas said, and if you were lucky to get it you could retire at the age of sixty-five and draw a pension of a couple shillings a week and never have to shovel another ball of horseshit for the rest of your life. A lovely prospect to outline to a kid of fifteen. However, the motorcar put paid to that dream, as motorcars do not shit on the street the way that horses do.

In the midst of all this future talk, a miracle happened: the Carnegie Library came to Limerick and opened my mind to a wide magical world beyond the gray puritan confines of our benighted city, with endless possibilities of vibrant life and adventure. My brothers and myself devoured books. We were hungry for the words, with warnings from various vigilante grown-ups that we were going to ruin our eyes with all that reading, but they were in dread of us finding out the hypocrisy of our community. There were not a lot of new books in the library, as most of their stock was donated and what an eclectic collection it was. The librarians were not trained folk as in the United States, as they seemed to share two hatreds: books and children. They made borrowing books difficult and made us go away to wash our filthy hands even if they were clean.

These so-called librarians were just relations of local politicians who needed a cushy job inside, out of the elements. But once we got inside, it was heaven. We rapidly got through the kids' sections and progressed to the grown-up section and got books from there on the pretext that they were for a relative. There was a fee to join the library and, small as it was, it was a hardship for my mother, but the authorities made no allowance for the poor and it appeared that they would just as soon we stayed away because poor people with knowledge were a menace to a corrupt government.

For me, reading led to dreaming and dreaming interfered with attention to school work, with its stodgy curriculum of rote & repetition, and enlivened by the infliction of the corporal punishment so common in those days. Sometimes it was for something as minor as a blot of ink on your copy book, as there were no ballpoints in those days, and the old nibs often dropped blobs on the paper. I dreamt of warm clothes, of a house with electricity full of books so that I could read in bed at night. I dreamt of having a loving mother and father who were cheery and encouraging, and I dreamt of having a bed that didn't stink of piss and shit, with a soft pillow and lovely white sheets on an uncollapsed mattress, and the bedside lamp.

What did I think then of what was going to happen in my life? One job I wanted was as a bellboy in a local hotel, which was the most fashionable place in town. I thought I would get to meet all kinds of interesting people and they would recognize in me such qualities of intellect they would offer to take me to America, the land of my birth, and launch me on a highly successful career. That did not happen. I joined the Irish Army at age fourteen to learn music but was thrown out at age fifteen for lack of aptitude for music they said and off I went to England to work as a factory hand in Dunlop's bike factory. I lived in a boardinghouse with a huge crew of Irish laborers, many of them alcoholics, a few communists, but all vital and lively talkers. There were other boardinghouses on that street with signs in their windows: Rooms to Let—No Irish or Animals! Please! The English are so polite they even say please to the animals and to the savage Irish. A few years of laboring in Coventry and managing to get to London for some theater and concerts, plus the revitalizing visits to the public library, saving me from going cuckoo and always illuminating my life's path, such as it was.

I got back to Limerick still gloomy and despairing both of us, man and city, but I was informed that the local theater company was seeking members, so that gave me hope, as I'd aspirations in that department. It did not take me long to ascertain the name of the man in charge of this theater crowd and off I went to see him. I did not have the necessary wardrobe of the aspiring thespian, but I got as neat as I could, combed my unruly mop. But of course I was still obviously from the slums, no hiding that, so when I entered the august presence of the eminence in charge, he put his fingertips together, looked at me from over his spectacles with all the warmth of a man seeing a rat regurgitating his dinner. "Yesssssssss!" he said, the word sounding like a displeased cobra.

"I would like to join the College Players," I said.

"What for?" he replied.

"I would like to be an actor."

"What makes you think you could be an actor?"

"Because I want to be one, sir."

"Hmm! If ever we need anyone of your type, we will send for you, good day," dismissing me with a wave toward the door.

As always, I heard what I wanted to hear (i.e., We will send for you!). It was raining outside when I left, but I did not care. I splashed through puddles, sang snatches of songs, recited bits of doggerel verse, leapt and jumped through the downpour and got home so rapidly that I thought I must have sprouted the wings of angels. When the euphoria of the "being sent for" line evaporated, the serpent of reality began to uncoil itself in my soul. One obvious mistake was, how could anyone send for you if they had not asked for or been given your address? There were no telephones available in slum dwellings, indeed no electric light, not even a number on the door for them to find me. That incident occurred over fifty years ago, and I am sure that theater eminence has, as they say, gone to his reward, but I never heard from him, nor did the College Players ever ask me to be even a part of crowd scene. Now, dream killing is not yet a criminal offense, but people who murder young people's dreams ought to be sentenced to one week's confinement in a cell, with only a rabid conservative for company.

The next job in Limerick was as a houseboy in a residence for Jesuit priests. All I had to do there was sweep floors, shine up the linoleum, polish the priests' shoes, and answer the door when the folk came looking for a priest . . . and to look as holy as possible. For the princely sum of about two dollars a week, I worked ten hours a day, six days a week, but we houseboys ate well, as the priests were all hearty trenchermen, and there was no stinting of the viands or the vino, or of the cognacs, the ports, the sherries, and on all days there were plenty of left-overs. It was all very classy—real silver cutlery, gold-rimmed dinnerware, and all the decanters and glasses were pure crystal long before we were warned about the lead content of crystal. All the gleaming of the white table linen, the beauty of the fresh flowers, and everything on those tables gave rise to more dreaming. Someday . . . someday . . . I will get to sit at some banquet tables and be the equal of all who sit there. I will know about the courses, which knife and fork to use, and I will discourse on the wine and its vintage. I will know to cross the knife and fork to indicate my meal is not yet finished, or to lay them side by side to show I am done. I will know to call the napkin a serviette, as only common people call it a napkin, and to dab my mouth rather than rub it, etc. etc.

My brother Frank saved his money and sez he extracted a large sum of money from the bosom of a dead moneylender to help pay his fare to America. He'd done some collecting for said dead moneylender. It was not long before he sent me the fare to join him here, but he had gone in the army by the time I got here. It was a luxurious voyage, six days of sumptuous dinners, lunches, room service all night; the dreams were starting to come true.

The Manhattan skyline hove into view, and as we sailed past the Statue of Liberty a lump came in my throat as I looked at that icon of hope for the world, and I can safely say I have not met anyone who was not moved as I was by that sight. But dreams soon get grounded in reality, as my first job was as a dishwasher, second job was answering phones in the service, third job inspecting concrete on the Jersey Turnpike extension to the Holland Tunnel; next was working on the docks as a longshoreman, and then loading trucks in a warehouse. At night I drank and other times I went to the theater. One night, after seeing a powerful Synge play, I screwed up my courage and went backstage and spoke to a producer about becoming an actor. My lack of experience did not faze him and he hired me to appear off-Broadway in the play, as someone was leaving the cast, and that was the beginning of my stage career. Then it was press interviews, and a producer for the *Tonight Show*, hosted by Jack Paar, was intrigued by how I got the job, so he booked me on the show. I had a lot to drink prior to going on, but they said I was hilarious, so I was asked back often.

A saloon that I drank in was shorthanded, so they asked me to get behind the bar and help out and, because of the notoriety brought on by the *Tonight Show*, a couple of guys asked me to open up a saloon bearing my name, and so came the first singles bar in New York (indeed, if not in the United States). So here I was, having barely landed in the United States with actually four dollars in my kick, and I am some sort of minor big deal appearing on stage, on television, and lording it over the masses in a saloon called Malachy's. King of the Castle, I thought in my arrogance, but pride cometh before the fall.

A hasty marriage based on a very liquid foundation collapsed in an acrimonious divorce, toppled me from my throne, and, after a few years of immersion in alcohol, I got married to my present friend and spouse, Diana. It was a long time before sobriety took hold after adventures in India, Africa, and all of Europe, but a steady marriage, a plentitude of love in my life, fairly steady work in the business of show quieted my restive spirit, plus the reality of dreams coming true because I helped my dreams and fostered them, rather than indulge in destruction, as I had previously.

I was always ashamed of not having a formal education, so when people would say *You should write a book*, I always managed to joke my way out of it. Who would give a fiddler's fart for my thoughts, my opinions, or my idiotic empty life? You can take the child out of the slum but you can't take the slum out of the child. The prime element in poverty is the absence of self-esteem, and, no matter how well we poverty-class people do, we are always plagued with the thought *I am not worthy of this*, so what have I accomplished?

Got to America (courtesy of my brother). Became an actor (by luck). Opened up a saloon (with other people's money). Got on television (through a friend). Got married to a young woman (who thought I was a somebody). And so I never could take credit for anything I did, it was always luck, chance, or influence. Eventually I did get to write a book after *Angela's Ashes* was a big hit, but it has stood on its own merits and was a *New York Times* best seller, plus I was asked to be the Green Party candidate for governor of New York, all of which has helped me realize I do have talent, I do deserve some of the rewards for my efforts in living a good life, and that life is not all chance.

Am I where I thought I would be years ago? No! I am so far ahead of my dreams that I could die this night with just a few regrets. Here I am, seventy-seven years of age, happily married to Diana for forty-four years. We have five children between us and five grandchildren. I am on loving terms with my brothers Frank, Mike, and Alphie, who has just published his first book. I am at peace with most of the human race, still working as an actor, a recognized author, there's no nicotine in my life, alcohol has been out for over twenty-four years, and my health is quite good, thank you.

I have seen a good deal of our world, met & talked to some of the grandest people you could ever hope to meet, and I remember my nights now and what I said, and I don't say things that I have to apologize for, and I remember what made me laugh, too. I am on the road facing the light in search of another dream. And as I am wont to say: Live every day as if it is going to be your last because one day you will be right.

MALACHY MCCOURT is a Brooklyn-born, Limerick-reared author and raconteur who has been a longshoreman, radio personality, playwright, actor, and, in 2006, a New York gubernatorial candidate. He is the author of *A Monk Swimming*, which earned best-seller status in the United States and abroad, *Singing My Him Song*, *Bush Lies in State*, *Malachy McCourt's History of Ireland*, *Through Irish Eyes: A Visual Companion to Angela McCourt's Ireland*, *The Claddagh Ring: Ireland's Cherished Symbol of Friendship, Loyalty and Love*, *Harold Be Thy Name: Lighthearted Daily Reflections for People in Recovery*, and two books in collaboration: *The McCourts of New York* and *The McCourts of Limerick*.

VICKI TOPAZ

THE RABBIT'S TATTOO

Margot Beth Duxler

(For Heidi)

In a cottage in a wood,
Little man by the window stood,
Saw a rabbit hopping by, knocking at the
door.
Help me! Help me! Help, she said,
Before the hunter shoots me dead!
Little rabbit come inside,
Safely you'll abide.

—Anonymous

The way I can tell how I really feel is by listening to the music in my head. Something's always playing. Sometimes, being me is like being on an elevator that's stuck between floors: Muzak with way too much treble blaring endlessly through invisible speakers. Other times, I have the best seat in the house for a private performance of my favorite artists.

Since before I can remember, my auditory cortex has provided musical accompaniment for all sorts of events in my life. Not the kind of music from an errant radio wave that vibrates in a mercury-infused gold filling and prompts the sartorial splendor of a tinfoil hat. This music comes from somewhere inside my unconscious, narrating, editorializing, often with cutting irony. From the moment my brother called to tell me that our mother had died, and then, during the long standby wait at the San Francisco airport, and the four-hour red-eye to Chicago, the constant background accompaniment to the numbing, mechanical, foreground fog was Bob Dylan's "Stuck Inside of Mobile," the chorus repeatedly asking if this can really be the end. The perfect lament for a filial relationship that never had a shot at being resolved. And when I finally graduated from decades of psychotherapy, all I heard for weeks before my last session was "I'll See You in My Dreams." It even made my analyst laugh.

During a period when my home address was House of Cynics c/o the Black Hole of Self-Loathing, I recalled that saccharin-tasting platitude *It's never too late to have a happy childhood*, which propelled me at warp speed to a memory that had been dimly twinkling, light-years away. I was three years old. I know because we lived in Chicago at Irving Park and Clarendon, and I was sitting by the window that over-looked the green-grass yard of the apartment complex next door. Our building only had a paved courtyard. I was playing with the buttons in my mother's sewing box, an old candy tin that to this day retains the lingering fragrance of the caramels it once held. The sparkly buttons were fairies and the little round cloth-covered buttons were cats and dogs, and the big brass and wooden buttons were vampires. They all lived in my Amber Forest, which consisted of four large flower pots planted with variegated coleus, and it was amazing how the adventures and misadventures of this little kingdom paralleled my own. If one of the baby fairies had a big bruise on her arm from being bitten by a vampire, you could be sure that I had a paternally produced punch-bruise in the corresponding spot on my arm. One time, the mother fairy refused to allow one of her daughters to attend the fairy tea party because the girl was so fat she could barely fly, which occurred, remarkably, right after my mother had wept with embarrassment when the saleslady at Belles and Beaux Clothing for Children said I needed a dress from the *chubby* department if I wanted to be able to zip it up.

That was the first time I remember music coming to help me understand what I didn't yet have words for. A few days earlier, it had poured in on invisible waves through the open window of our upstairs neighbor's kitchen and straight into my crypto brain-recording device. *Mama may have, and Papa may have, but God bless the child that's got his own.* The song returned to rescue me like a mama cat seizing her kitten by the scruff of its neck just in time to save it from the jaws of a charging pit bull. Then and there I made a vow, a promise to myself that when I grew up I'd always remember what it was like to be a child. I'd never hurt my children and boot-stomp their happiness or make them ashamed and filled with bilious poison. I swore I would never forget.

Over the years, most of the musical messages I've received

have been clear, but sometimes the tunes can seem random and the meaning of the music more difficult to decipher. If I pay attention, however, it becomes obvious that, like dreams, the music is trying to enlighten me, force me to pay attention, even if it requires hitting me upside the head with a melodic and lyrical two-by-four. For example, I recently found myself listening to Steve Earle's poignant duet with his sister, "When I Fall," only to realize days later that I had been worried about my friend Harriet, who had fallen at work, smashed her patella, and almost died when a rogue blood clot lodged in her lung. I felt more anxious than I could tolerate knowing, until the song brought my fear and worry into full awareness: the trepidation of losing a loved one and the enormous relief of reprieve. Another bullet dodged.

The good news is that it's impossible to be in denial when you have a personal life-events soundtrack in your head. The bad news is that it's impossible to be in denial when you have a personal life-events soundtrack in your head.

Ten years ago, I turned fifty to the melodies of Springsteen's "Born to Run," Bette Midler's "Do You Wanna Dance?" and Golden Bough's "The Star of the County Down." Turning sixty has been a very different story. For one thing, I've already flirted with mortality, having had open-heart surgery at fifty-five to remove a tumor from my left atrium. And a few months ago, my thyroid quit on me without so much as two weeks' notice. It doesn't help that neither of my parents lived to see sixty-five, a family tradition I do not wish to continue.

I greeted this sixtieth-birthday milestone in the company of Joni Mitchell's "Circle Game" on the turntable, experiencing the hopelessness of my efforts to decelerate time itself. The day before my birthday, while I was cleaning the moldy grout in the shower, Judy Collins was singing "Who Knows Where the Time Goes?" which my joker of a warped mind fun-house-mirrored into "Who Knows Where the Slime Grows?" If turning fifty was "Yea!" then turning sixty has been "Oh, shit!" accompanied by that obnoxious *60 Minutes* clock tick-tick-ticking away and insisting that I ponder all manner of things one ponders upon failing miserably to deny the reality of aging and the inevitable event that follows, known at my house as the *D-word*.

I'm aware that my days are numbered, and I want to spend them attentively, fully. Certainly, there are places I want to see before I die, things I want to do, but the epidemic of so-called *bucket list books* that are reproducing like the Ebola virus are about as appealing as gum surgery: *A Thousand Things to See, Do, Visit, Eat, before You Die.* The last thing I want is for my life to become a checklist for a game of *Beat the Reaper.* I would like to acknowledge the fact of the final curtain with dignity and wisdom, not cowering in a corner or frantically trying to pack it all in like a deranged golden retriever with six tennis balls in its mouth.

I'm old enough to know that more is not necessarily better, but I also don't want to miss the opportunity of a lifetime because I haven't been paying attention.

Initially, when that Cottage in the Wood song started up on my internal iPod—apparently set on endless repeat—I had no clue what to make of it. Begin my second childhood? Make a contribution to the SPCA? In truth, I'm still adequately *compos mentis* to instantly associate any reference to rabbits, bunnies, or hares with Heidi, primarily known as The Rabbit, the teenager who changed my life when I was twenty-nine. So while I made the connection to Rabbit, I couldn't understand *what* about her I needed to figure out. Then, on the evening of my Aunt Harriet's yarzheit (Harriets have always had a special place in my life)—she died two years ago, at the age of eighty-eight—the cloying little tune began to make sense.

Aunt Harriet and I were closer than my mother and I had ever been, and I was very lucky to be able to be with her the last week of her life to sing with her, hold her, tell her how much I loved her, say good-bye, and ask her to please put in a good word for me with the parents. We sang the songs that her mother had sung to her when she was a child, and that she in turn had sung to me. On the charts with a bullet were "Blow Wind, Blow," an old nursery rhyme whose origins are long lost, and "Won't You Come Over to My House?" which was an absolutely maudlin tune by the early twentieth-century duo of Van Alstyne & Williams about a bereaved mother who befriends a lonely little girl.

What touched me most about those remaining days we spent together was a conversation she had with my husband, Michael, shortly before she slipped away. He had asked her to tell him the most difficult thing about dying, and her first response was a typical Aunt Harriet wisecrack, "You'll find out!" But then she thought about the question and answered from her heart, "It's leaving the people you love."

As I lit the candle to honor and remember her, an image of that scene returned to me: Michael sitting in a chair beside her hospital bed, holding one of her manicured hands; me on the bed holding the other hand, the simple truth of her words pulsing through us. She pressed our palms to emphasize her point, and Michael and I reached across her and intertwined our fingers, completing our connection. *Will the circle be unbroken? Bye and bye, Lord, bye and bye.* And suddenly, I knew what the camp and campy Cottage in the Wood song was trying to tell me: Remember *God Bless the Child* and the vow I made. Remember my promise to never forget how deeply a child can be hurt. Before I start pushing up daisies, I need to make things right with my Rabbit.

Many years ago—when cable car and bus fare were twenty-five cents and the Eagle Cafe was at sea level, feeding sailors and longshoremen, and not on the second level of Pier 39 and serving tourists; those years before global warming and four-dollar coffee and studio apartments renting for $1,800 a month—I was twenty-nine, and two very important events changed my life. First, I decided not to kill myself; second, I requested and obtained legal custody of a sixteen-year-old girl: Heidi.

The first event is pretty self-explanatory. I still had hope that the debilitating depression that had sickened me since childhood could be neutralized. Instead of lugging all my past garbage around and contaminating the present and the future, maybe I could learn to compost it and use it as fertilizer to enrich my life. Some spark of hope, in the person of my uncannily prescient therapist, enabled me to take a chance. With great patience and perseverance, she taught me the ancient art of emotional alchemy: turning shit into manure.

The second phenomenon—the legal custody of Heidi—is much more complicated. I had been friends with Heidi and her family since she was twelve. I loved her the way you love a cat or dog—or a rabbit, for that matter: without conflict or confusion. Just flat-out love, no questions asked. But then, she was easy to love. She was an adorable, coltish adolescent, slipping on and off the balance beam between childhood dependence and neo-adult independence. What made her irresistible, though, was perceptible indirectly: unspoken and intuited. As Antoine de Saint-Exupery opined in *The Little Prince*, "It is only with the heart that one can rightly see. What is essential is invisible to the eye." And that's how it was between us: love that was felt, tacitly acknowledged, never named.

Heidi had adapted to the chaos and neglect in her life by becoming ultra-competent, stoic, never asking for help. In spite of her protective thorns, her sensitivity and longing for connection were transparent. What she couldn't say was what I heard, and it made me want to shelter and protect her. I had to be careful though. A direct declaration of "I love you" was likely to be met with "You'll get over it!"

Coming to live with me seemed like a natural next step when her mother's marriage to her stepfather was going off the rails and Heidi, her siblings, and step-siblings were shooting off in all directions. A real nuclear family meltdown, complete with toxic fallout. Her mother, Betty, was particularly eccentric and had decided that she was going to make her fortune selling American jeans on the black market in Yugoslavia. She assumed that if she couldn't find someone for Heidi to live with, she would take her out of school and bring her along. It didn't seem to matter to her that Heidi was attending Lowell, the top public advanced-placement high school in San Francisco, which would almost guarantee her acceptance at any college of her choice.

Heidi's stepfather, Bob, was responsible for three children from a previous marriage and would have been happy to keep Heidi with him, but he couldn't afford another mouth at the table. It seemed that her only choice was to drop out of school and go with her mother. Or so she thought. She never asked me. Heidi never would have asked me. But when I suggested that she live with me while her mother was out of the country, she didn't ponder the question. Betty and I signed papers making me Heidi's legal guardian, and Betty took off for Eastern Europe, looking for her pot of gold. So Heidi, soon to become *The Rabbit*, moved in with my roommate, Ron, and me in a shoebox-sized apartment in an alley behind Saints Peter and Paul Church in North Beach.

Heidi earned her moniker after she and I had seen the animated adaptation of Richard Adams's book *Watership Down*. It's an epic adventure about a colony of rabbits forced to seek a new home because developers are taking over their sylvan paradise to build a subdivision. There's a seagull in the movie, whose voice was created by the late Zero Mostel, and whenever he was irritated with any of the bunnies, he'd screech, "Stupid rabbit!" After the film, Heidi and I walked home squawking, "Stupid rabbit!" at each other. I must have squawked more insistently because the nickname stuck to her in all its permutations and evolutions: Rabbit, Bunny, Bunz, Bunnybutt, Bunzilla, etc. The variations were endless. And it's the Law of Nicknames that when you love someone, using his or her *real* name is okay only if you're angry. Otherwise, it's too distant. Too formal. Think about it. Would you ever call out, "Lovey, come up here and clean up this mess!" Of course not. You'd be more likely to launch every name on the birth certificate and some expletives to boot.

The three of us—Rabbit, Ron, and I—were quite the *all-un-American family*. Ron had moved in shortly before Rabbit, after his girlfriend had broken up with him. One rainy night he called from a phone booth, having had so much to drink that he didn't know where he was. When I asked him to poke his head out and give me street sign coordinates so I could pick him up, he insisted he was at the corner of Telephone and Telephone.

"Drop the receiver and look at a *street* sign, you moron," I yelled. "And then don't budge until I get there!"

Of course, Rabbit and I never let Ron forget this episode. It became part of our defining creation story. In our more sadistic moods, we could bring Ron to hysterical laughter just by whispering, "Can you give me the cross streets . . . ?" or "It was a dark and stormy night . . ."

United by design rather than blood, our ragged little crew made a life. Perhaps it appeared that we were randomly thrown together. But it was something larger and luckier than that: we had chosen each other as family.

Now that I'm clear about what the Cottage in the Wood song means, I have to tell Rabbit a couple of things before the sands run out. The first one is that the door code is in a Ziploc bag under the flower pot by the garage door. Okay, seriously. I just don't want any more time to go by because, after finding my car keys in the freezer (at least the ice cream was there, too, and not in my purse), I just can't be sure what little jokes my memory has in store down the line.

When people find out that when I was twenty-nine I was responsible for a sixteen-year-old girl, their usual reaction is along the lines of "Oh, how generous, what a great gesture." I may have provided the physical space, but it was Rabbit who made it a home during a time in my life when I was demonically depressed and scrambling to back away from the abyss before the ground gave way. She was the one who was responsible (except when I didn't know she wasn't), hardworking, smart as a whip, completely adorable, and dangerously funny. The queen of deadly timing. She always delivered a punch line at just the right moment to ensure a wine-out-the-nose laugh or the aspiration of a chocolate chip cookie. And smart funny, too. Ironic, rather than knock-knock.

I couldn't quite imagine what it was like for her that her mother was in Yugoslavia for who-knew-how-long, her father was living in Florida, and her sister, brother, stepfather, and step-siblings were scattered to the winds. I knew I didn't want to be another undependable-presumed grown-up.

The revelation of a tattoo can be enlightening. Years after the fact, when Rabbit showed me the red heart with its single wing raised in flight that decorated her left hipbone, I was shocked. It was the kind of shock that clarifies, decodes, and redefines. Like one of those pictures so popular some years ago where, if you looked directly at them, all that was visible was an abstract amalgam of lines, but if you relaxed your gaze and looked slightly away, the seemingly random components suddenly reorganized into a recognizable three-dimensional image. Epiphany!

When Rabbit finally exposed her tattoo, we were having dinner at her house and she was, if memory serves, twenty-two. I remember that naughty-bunny grin as she sauntered over to me while unzipping her jeans. "I have something to show you," she said, obviously thrilled by the bemusement and discomfort on my face. She folded back the denim to display the perfect red heart with its single yellow, blue, and black wing. I think I screamed. I know she laughed.

"When did you get that?" I sputtered

"After I moved in with you," she said, grinning.

How she had managed to keep it a secret in that tiny apartment, with both of us prone to walking around half-dressed, I'll never know. On one level, I was astonished that she was so clever at hiding it from me. She must have strategically draped her after-bath towels, or covered the tattoo with a seemingly naturally placed hand. I never had a clue. But on a deeper level, I became aware that, in keeping from me something I disapproved of, she was actually protecting me. It was as if she knew instinctively that I would have felt helpless with this fait accompli, and that I'd also be mortified because, previously, I'd so freely expressed my opinion of tattoo aficionados as lowlifes, drunks, and idiots.

Before the tattoo revelation, I, of course, knew how much I loved Rabbit, but I don't think I realized just how much she totally understood me and, in her subtle, invisible way, took care of me. I never felt that she was merely trying to get away with something. That may have been part of it, but I think the larger motivation was to keep me from worrying about her and what it meant if I knew that she had a permanent inscription in her flesh.

I also think she hid it because she refused to let anyone else define her, a quality that makes her unabashedly curious, authentic, open-minded, and, paradoxically, stubborn. People are so wrong to think I did her a good turn: she was my rudder and compass. As well as my wise-ass, of course. I wish I had taken care of her with the same grace with which she took care of me.

I must be feeling something similar to what my Twelve Step patients feel when they begin the Fourth Step of taking a "searching and fearless moral inventory" and making amends. My memory is conveniently fuzzy when I try to recall exactly what happened when Rabbit left our place and went to live at the Russian River. In fact, my memory of that time is more like a shredder, making it impossible for me to reconstruct the chronology of events and feelings. Dylan Thomas couldn't remember whether it snowed for six days and six nights when he was twelve, or whether it snowed for twelve days and twelve nights when he was six. His was a literary device; I have no excuse.

What I know: Rabbit was leaving. She was nineteen and had friends who lived there. She was trying out her wings.

What I don't know: Was she going for the summer? Or forever.

What I did: The minute she was gone, I set up shoji screens in her room, covering the artwork on her walls, the clothing she had left and, ultimately, all traces of her presence.

What happened next: A painful demonstration of how unconscious acts can have unintended consequences. Not an hour after she left, Rabbit came back unexpectedly to pick up something she had forgotten. She walked into her room and her face said it all: Expelled. Shunned. Disappeared. I had made her invisible. My betrayal was all the more paradoxical because it wasn't born of wanting her gone, but of my conflict about her leaving and my attachment to her. In a seriously stupid act, I was attempting to manage my feelings of loss by hiding all reminders of those feelings.

God Bless the Child. I had forgotten my vow. My promise to remember the vulnerability of a developing soul. I had failed us both.

Rabbit has never mentioned what happened. We've had a conspiracy of silence. I've spent three cowardly decades, thirty circles around the sun ineffectively avoiding the whole incident. I'm fortunate not to have an undertow of regrets in my life pulling me out to sea. There are not many things about my past that I'd like to go back to and change. But if I could undo what I did to Rabbit that day, I'd gladly be reincarnated as an amoeba and start my entire evolution from scratch. *Sorry* doesn't do justice to the regret I feel. It won't change what happened, but it's all I have at hand to shovel up that piece of our history and toss it in with the rest of the compost. There's still a lot of planting we can do together.

You know how pregnant women see babies everywhere, and cat lovers spot felines behind every window curtain? I'm sitting at my desk, steeped in memories of Rabbit and Ron and the church bells of Saints Peter and Paul waking us on an early Sunday morning, and all of a sudden I look up and realize that for fifteen years I've had a lithograph hanging above my desk of two rabbits sitting in a moonlit grove. The last birthday card I bought was a reproduction of the Dürer print *The Young Hare.* These days, I'm noticing rabbits everywhere.

A licensed clinical psychologist in private practice in San Francisco, Dr. **MARGOT BETH DUXLER** is the author of the psycho-biography *Seduction: A Portrait of Anais Nin* (Edgework Books). Her fiction has appeared in a number of literary journals and in the anthology *For Keeps*. With W. A. Smith, she served as coeditor of fiction for the *Five Fingers Review*; with Edouard Muller, she worked as cotranslator for the first edition of *Gault-Millau's The Best of Paris*. She is a professional fiddler and has performed and recorded with Golden Bough and the Celtic Wonder Band. Duxler is currently working on a novel and a collection of short stories.

ROGER McGUINN

CLARA

Kathi Kamen Goldmark

Over the last few months, there have been moments when I've glanced at myself in the mirror and a trick of the light has turned my reflection, with this new bit of softness around the jaw and eyes, into Clara. When she first appeared in the mirror, I banished her with a change of angle or expression, perceiving the resemblance as an optical illusion, a betrayal of my own bone structure and skin tone. Even though she always looked young for her age, even though I adored her, this would not do. There is absolutely no possible way I could be old enough to look like my grandmother.

When I was starting school (and she was younger than I am now), she combed out my long, wavy hair. "What do you want to be when you grow up?" The question was meant to distract me from the discomfort of her wet comb pulling through the tangles.

"A ballerina and a nurse!" I declared decisively. Cherry Ames, student nurse, was my favorite fictional character at the time—Helen Wells, whoever she was, couldn't crank out those books fast enough for me. And I'd recently seen *Swan Lake* and had fallen in love with the grace and beauty of the dancers.

"And a mommy, too!" Harder to articulate was a desire to create and enjoy my own vivid world of people and places, independent but connected to my family, and *mommy* was the closest I could get.

Even then, Clara must have known that she had possibly the klutziest granddaughter in the universe (I routinely turned left half a beat after all the other little girls in Mrs. Costigan's ballet class turned right), as well as the most squeamish when it came to the sight of blood, but she never skipped a beat.

"You can be anything in the world you want to be, *shana maidela*, anything at all," she insisted, using the Yiddish term that, literally translated, means *pretty girl*. Coming out of the mouth of your grandma, it means a whole lot more, somehow including love, expectation, and wedding china.

Clara didn't really have the "you can be anything at all" option herself. She was born in 1902, moved from the Ukraine with her family when she was a baby, and grew up street-smart and fearless in New York, tagging along after a pack of older brothers. But she also loved school and was heartbroken when she had to quit at fourteen to help support her family. Bright but inadequately educated, Clara let go of a few of her own dreams. As a young bride, she perfected the Depression-era art of preparing delicious meals out of a potato and an onion; she raised two daughters and dressed them in home-made finery; she learned how to take bits of shirt cardboard and library paste and turn them into fanciful toys. As times improved, Clara's taste became more "modren" (her pronunciation of the word). She bought wall-to-wall carpeting to replace her elegant but old and worn Persian rug. She dressed in color-coordinated pantsuits and gold jewelry, and she became a blonde who was never seen in public without eight pounds of blue eye shadow—she once checked herself out of an ICU to take a subway to Bloomingdale's because they didn't carry her brand of makeup in the hospital gift shop. She had her own sense of style and an eye for what looked good on others. When it was time to buy my school clothes, we'd hit the department stores and bring our haul home for alterations, where she'd add a ribbon here, change a hem there, making each outfit unique. Leftover fabric turned into matching dresses for my dolls.

Later on, my grandmother was the first to come up with loot like training bras and pantyhose, as well as a rather shocking thirteenth-birthday gift. When I opened her present, I expected a porcelain doll or a charm for my gold bracelet; anything but the red-lace lingerie I found nestled in pastel tissue paper.

"You should always remember, *mamelah*, that the boys like to see a little panty every once in a while," was her mysti-fying explanation. My mother, who'd put some genuine effort into making sure my panties were tastefully covered at all times, looked a little startled. And I (a girl who still sometimes arranged the occasional secret rendezvous with an old box of Barbie dolls in the basement) didn't quite comprehend what Clara was getting at, especially when my older cousin Alice started giggling. It was just one more adult mystery to be filed in the same brain-space as jokes that ended with Yiddish punch lines or words I couldn't find in the dictionary.

Along with the insistence that I could be anything I wanted to be (except—ever more obviously as time went on—a ballerina) was the message that I was supposed to look "gawgeous" in order to attract a husband, and she assumed I would end up comfortably married to a successful man. This grandmother, who would give me anything within her power to give, let it be known that she was holding something back until that magical event occurred. My favorite item in her kitchen, an odd little gadget designed to slice hard-boiled eggs, would not be handed over until my wedding day.

But as the years rolled by, I grew less interested in Clara's fashion and dating tips. Pretty outfits languished in the closet as I devised sneaky ways to change from my high school skirt-and-sweater set into jeans on the Long Island Railroad, as I set off to spend lazy Saturdays in Greenwich Village nursing café mochas and playing checkers with self-described existentialists. My career goals changed, along with my clothing and friends. No longer the wanna-be ballerina/nurse, I longed to become a world-renowned folksinger like Joan Baez or Judy Collins. Actually, I didn't want to be *like* Joan or Judy, I wanted to *be* them—both of them at the same time, if possible.

I learned enough guitar to accompany myself through a set of sincere soprano warbling topped off by my personal show-stopper, "The Cat Came Back," and started performing around our tiny Long Island community. There was always a hootenanny looking for the likes of me, and I got a respectable number of gigs (a couple of them even paid!) under my belt before heading off to that bastion of leftie politics, Quaker tradition, and hippie subculture called Antioch College.

The first big shock came when I realized I wasn't the only

sweet-voiced girl gunning to be the next Joanie and/or Judy, and some of the others were damn good. I developed a virulent strain of "chick-singer-itis," a malady that strikes young female musicians with an insatiable craving to be the one and only. A solo act on the high school hootenanny circuit, I had no experience at musical collaboration—and also no stomach for competition. I backed off, put my guitar away, and found other diversions.

It turned out there were all sorts of worthy causes in need of my energy and skills, and even though in those days the girls were mostly relegated to flyer-stapling and joint-rolling duty, the heady atmosphere of the anti-war movement was addictive. I was drawn to the budding SDS (Students for a Democratic Society) group on campus, the small activist radio station (where I joined the cast of a Saturday morning stoner/kiddie show called "Orange Banana Balloon" that aired between Jefferson Airplane tracks and political diatribe). I went on marches, armed with handkerchiefs soaked in baking-soda solution and a motorcycle helmet, ready for tear gas and the clubbing of over-enthusiastic cops. I listened to my friends and acquaintances give speeches. When Robin Morgan took the podium at a huge national anti-war demonstration and belted out a rousing feminist call to action, my boyfriend of the moment scolded me for not participating in her standing ovation. Talk about damned if you do and damned if you don't . . .

More than anyone else in my family, Clara seemed to understand why these events were crucial. She told me stories about going to secret meetings in The Village (always somehow pronounced in capital letters) when sweatshops were being unionized, and about the dark-skinned Spanish boy she went all gooey over when she was seventeen. His name was Dilemmus, and he walked her home from the union meetings and courted her by playing the mandolin under her bedroom window. They fell madly in love and made plans to run away together, but she got cold feet. "I couldn't do this to my parents," she explained. "This was not the way of life." Clara married another suitor, a nice young Jewish man, my funny Grandpa Lou. But Dilemmus was used as a cautionary tale more than once: when I got tear-gassed at a rally, or when I brought an African American boyfriend home. She never forgot that first romance and saw Dilemmus reflected in the faces of my multiethnic college friends.

Then there was Antioch's version of the party life. Located in a tiny town in southwestern Ohio, we were a stopping-off point for hippies traveling from one coast to the other, and our community—though out in the middle of nowhere, with a one-block downtown and an adjacent nature preserve—felt pretty urban when it came to the accessibility of certain substances. It was easy to live in the moment, hanging out with my little tribe in patchouli-scented dorm rooms, selecting an interdisciplinary major and taking the classes that interested me, whether or not they fit any grand career scheme. At that point, my future plans were articulated vaguely as wanting to work with children and make a difference in the world. But there was always some guy or other influencing my decisions. Should I take my work-study quarter in Boston or Chicago? Chances are the choice would be based, at least partly, on whichever boy was enjoying a peek at my panties that semester.

And somehow, in all the festive madness of the late sixties and early seventies, I got a little mixed up about the difference between becoming something yourself and living through someone else by decorating his arm. Instead of applying the discipline required to pursue that musical career, I welcomed relationships with guys who were musicians. That's how, soon after graduation, I found myself moving to Los Angeles with my drummer boyfriend so he could be a rock star. Months later, he had a single climbing the charts as one of the original members of a group called Steely Dan, and I basked in the glow—enjoying the privileges and parties, but also feeling a little left out.

I taught drama and music at a tiny private school, while he toured the world in an up-and-coming rock band. It was clear there was room for only one musician in our household, and he had unquestionable dibs. So I gamely shifted gears back over to the "work with kids and do something good for the world" plan by day, while strutting around after hours in fabulous seventies-chic: tiny diaphanous blouses made of scarves, appliquéd jeans, and platform shoes. Clara was delighted that I'd given up that sloppy hippie look for a bit of glamour, however alternative, and came up with one last doll, complete with leather boots, fishnets, and a paisley dress, draped in a real fur coat.

Like Clara, I used my creativity any way I could, including writing lyrics for the school plays I directed, designing fanciful sets and scenery, even teaching the sex education class I was assigned because no one else would do it. I started a school folk-music sing-along group, came up with a "strategy games" math class in which the kids sat around playing poker and Go for hours on end, developed a drama curriculum for the preschoolers and the middle schoolers, and wrote songs for my students' special birthdays. In retrospect, I am sure I was insufferably cool, but at some point I think I must have noticed that I was acting out a scenario very much like Clara's: making the most of the traditional woman's role as stay-at-home partner and schoolteacher, rather than risking a crash by reaching for my very own star. At least the "work with kids" dream was being fulfilled—I could check that one off the list.

Then came my "do something good for the world" period when I landed a job with a nonprofit agency dedicated to educating the world about the dangers of unchecked population growth. My mission, should I choose to accept it, was—get this—to convince rock stars to record taped public service announcements about the importance of using birth control, and get the PSAs played on eight hundred rock radio stations. Well, there were also mission statements and fund-raising proposals and endless meetings, but basically I was hired to reel in those rock stars. And reel them in I did, with the help of some music business buddies and an alternative rock station in San Francisco, where I eventually moved. At one point, a PSA I'd coproduced won a CLEO award for the station; a year later (still in my twenties), I was invited to be a family-planning media consultant for a social service agency under the auspices of the Mexican government. I had an expense account, and one of the first things I did was take Clara out to a fancy lunch. Even though I signed my expense-account American Express voucher with a flourish, I found after leaving the restaurant that she'd stuffed the cash to pay for lunch into my coat pocket.

In an alternative, nonprofit sort of way, you could say my star was on the rise. But there was that one crucial item still left on Clara's list of dreams for me . . . until I got married at thirty-three. By then, I'd already collected an extended family of ex-lovers and their kids, most of whom—along with Clara and my parents and cousins and brothers—danced at my wedding. There is no word in the English language that means "someone you think of as your stepchild because you lived with their dad, even though you never actually got married and aren't together anymore," but there should be. I finally got that egg slicer, decorated with ribbons and bows.

Once again, goals shifted and changed. I developed the courage and commitment to start performing in bands, and although I never achieved Judy or Joanie stature, I found great satisfaction, delight, and ironic humor in my standard-issue bar band adventures. Working four-set gigs in grungy clubs was a surefire antidote to chick-singer-itis, and I declared myself cured as I sought out other women to work with, learning to sing harmony and share the spotlight, even—especially—if that light was just one bare bulb over a creaky bandstand.

I had a child, my son, Tony, and soon after began working in book publishing in a variety of jobs that ultimately came to include novelist, columnist, and essayist, but also involved many varieties of author care (check nurse, after all)—and I met and befriended some of the most celebrated and fascinating personalities in the world of twentieth-century American literature.

Thanks to my grandmother, I knew how to entertain a bored child at a long restaurant dinner by making up alphabet games and puzzles. As the mother of a little boy, I often forgot to carry Kleenex in my purse but always had crayons and paper. As a publishing professional, I found little bits of whimsy with which to construct a memorable media appearance or book tour, and wasn't above employing a certain flirtatious smile (panties dangled if never delivered) when needed to tame the crustiest literary lions.

In some ways, my life and career have been the equivalent of Clara's fanciful toys constructed out of shirt cardboard and library paste—I've run a nonprofit family-planning education program, been a consultant to the Mexican government, managed a costume shop, worked in many aspects of publishing, produced literary events and a national radio show, become a published novelist, written reviews and columns and essays and a joke book, performed as a country-western and rock musician, and worked in retail and as the world's worst waitress.

I've been married and divorced, have one biological son, a daughter-in-law, and six sort-of stepchildren (the oldest nearly thirty years older than the youngest), and a couple of honorary grandchildren. And although I never became a world-famous

folk-singing diva (it turned out those jobs were already taken),
I have performed as founder of the Rock Bottom Remainders,
under rock-star conditions with actual rock stars, one of
whom was Judy Collins, someone I now count as a friend.

Although I've never hit the jackpot financially, compared
to the old nurse/ballerina plan, it's been a far more interesting
and fun and weird and wonderful ride than I could ever have
predicted. A lifelong freelancer, I've enjoyed a career assem-
bled with bubblegum and spit, a bit of Clara's artistic sparkle,
and boatloads of denial about what doesn't make sense or
can't be done. I've tried to approach my relationships with a
similar spirit—so I guess you could say there's been a wild bit
of ballet involved, too, along with the hard-earned knowledge
that dreams most often come true in a kind of sideways and
rambling fashion, and that's not only okay, but sometimes
more fun.

On the cusp of sixty, the biggest surprise is that there's still
so much future to plan. Rather than feeling all settled in and
winding down, I'm working on projects, getting ideas that make
me jump up and down and cause others to run for cover, writing
books, even planning to get married again—the single most
hopeful and future-presumptive act I can imagine. Clara would
have been thrilled, and would have sent another egg slicer.

Going through some old papers recently, I found a letter
from Clara, sent shortly before my first wedding, in which she
tried to share some favorite recipes. She really didn't know
how to explain the amounts of ingredients to use since she did
everything by instinct and feel, and that—more than the
recipes themselves—is what I love most.

*You can make many fish cakes & then freeze after it is
cooked—I bake or broil—filet cod fish, use leftover vegetables
or steamed diced carrots, small onion, celery—when fish is
chopped then osterize all vegetables with an egg and add any*

bread crumbs or cereal or what have you & make patties. Enjoy.

I wish I can say more, we have to experiment and imagine . . .

These days, when I see Clara in the mirror, I try to find the saucy bravado to look her in the eye and invite her in, understanding that it's an honor to look like my grandmother—a woman who spoke in rhymed couplets after two whiskey sours, who wore her hair in braids long after she became a mother, who yodeled (quite well, I'm told) when she leaned outside to wash her upstairs windows.

I am nearly the age she was when I spent the most time with her, and she always looked fifteen years younger than she was anyway, but that's just the luck of the gene pool enhanced by the beauty products she learned to adore later in life. The world she grew up in is long gone—my mother often talks about how astounded she would have been by developments like e-mail and Costco—but her creativity, wit, and resourcefulness are here for the taking, and I've tried to take them as far as I could.

She was a funny, wise, open-minded woman, and her visits are a chance to dream of an unlimited future, while having the tangles combed out of my hair, to be reminded that when a bright-eyed boy plays the mandolin under your window, he likes to see a little panty every once in a while.

KATHI KAMEN GOLDMARK is the author of *And My Shoes Keep Walking Back to You*, a novel; coauthor of *The Great Rock & Roll Joke Book* and *Mid-Life Confidential: The Rock Bottom Remainders Tour America with Three Chords and an Attitude*; and has contributed essays to several anthologies.

With Sam Barry, she writes a monthly advice column in *Book-Page*, "The Author Enablers." Goldmark is founder and member of the all-author rock band, the Rock Bottom Remainders, president and janitor of "Don't Quit Your Day Job" Records, and author liaison for Book Group Expo. She is producer of the radio show *West Coast Live* and recipient of the 2008 Women's National Book Association Award. Her Web site is http://www.redroom.com/author/kathi-kamen-goldmark.

THE BEE'S KNEES

Christine Kehl O'Hagan

My mother had blue eyes and never liked them. The Doyle eyes were small, she said, the Doyle eyelids droopy. My father, who had a short-lived career as a shirt model, had big brown eyes, his lashes long and thick. Thank God, my mother often said, the Kehl eyes were the ones my children got. Years later, when I overheard my son's fiancée compliment my mother on her "pretty blue eyes," I felt bad, for I'd never noticed. "A mother's eyes are on her children," says a Lebanese proverb, "and her children's eyes are on the world."

On our last car ride together, when I was driving my mother from her Queens apartment to our Long Island house for a simple overnighter, and the clot about to claim her life beginning its ascent, my mother wriggled in her seat and looked over at me. "What?" I asked, thinking she'd finally tell me which of her secretly gay Irish cousins had once made a pass at her. (In a lifetime of telling stories, that was the one she never quite finished.)

"I always thought you had my blue eyes," Mom laughed, fixing her scarf, looking out the window.

That was eleven years ago (long before my droopy Doyle eyelids collapsed on top of my big Kehl eyes), and I remember how my heart sank.

"Just a little mistake," I thought, waiting for her to look at me again, laugh, a rueful shake of her head, but she said nothing. I couldn't understand it. My mother was only seventy-eight and, until that moment, had been very sharp. I'm not someone who sees the glass as either half-full or half-empty—I see the glass as broken, with shards stuck in my feet. Wherever I go, doom and gloom tag along, and often they stick me on the wrong train. The only useful advice I ever got from a shrink was to think of my life as a closed dresser, my worries one to a drawer. So I put Mom in the sock drawer and slammed it shut. Mom is healthy, I told myself, she has many years left. But I was wrong.

All she had left were hours.

I never imagined that, in less than a day, she'd fall from my kitchen chair, hit her head, and in a horrifying few seconds, die in my husband Patrick's arms.

I think of myself as sane—relatively speaking—and yet, as my mother lay dying, I wanted to turn away from her, crawling around the floor on my hands and knees, like Jackie on the back of that long-ago Dallas limousine, searching for my mother's stories, my mother's memories, my mother's voice.

All first-time parents expect their firstborns to be perfect, and for that, the "next-borns" owe us a debt of gratitude. We firstborns are the busy ones, breaking in new marriages, tumbling around on the living room rug with gorgeous young parents, Mama, Papa, Baby bears. (Unless, of course, it's the babysitter we remember, tumbling around on the rug with her boyfriend, like two bears in heat and, from the doorway, we're watching a sneak preview of the upcoming movie *Primal Scene*.)

When the firstborns lie, parents stagger backwards and fall into the nearest chair. When the next-borns lie, it's strictly go-to-your-room. Firstborns are dramatic and tend to punish themselves, guilty as all hell for "destroying the faith/trust" their parents had in them. Or maybe that was just me. Even tweaking the faith/trust my parents had in me meant four hours of my mother striding up and down the four feet of kitchen linoleum with her hands behind her back, like Darwin at the Scopes Monkey Trial. When I was fourteen, the one Salem menthol cigarette I stole from Mom's purse meant a three-hour Daniel Webster–like lecture from behind the open ironing board. (By the time my sister Pam came along, my mother smacked her with the dishtowel and called it a day.)

Go into any next-borns' bedrooms during an active punishment and you'll find them on their computers, online gambling, ordering nitrogen, talking dirty to cops pretending to be cheerleaders. The parents barely notice. They're at the window, standing near the overhead projector, all set up for a PowerPoint presentation, waiting for the firstborn who has either lost her gloves, forgotten to pay a library fine, or dented a fender, thus breaking not only *their* hearts but the very Heart of God Himself.

I was born about a thousand years ago to the world's most mismatched couple. My mother was red-haired and freckled. My father, black-haired and intense. ("Scarcely Irish," my grandmother Sadie said of the man who would become my father. "A black-hearted, Eyetalian Protestant." And those were the *good* things.)

My mother read Shakespeare. My father read racing scores. She went to the theater. He went to the movies. She saw Laurence Olivier on Broadway. He saw Tom Mix in Keith's Flushing Theater. She took the subway, or the bus. He drove a Harley—once, through the front door of Duffy's Tavern in Flushing, after which he was banned for life. She didn't drink. He drank enough for both of them. She came from an Irish family where humor was both blessing and weapon. For a while, there was a piano. There was always song. He and his sister were orphans. They lived with their ancient grandmother, Lizzie, who knew the King James Bible, chapter and verse. My mother came from an apartment. She never lived in a house. My father never lived in an apartment. He and his sister lived in a series of big old houses with no closets.

After Dad's parents died, Grandma Lizzie took in borders, silent men passing through the silent rooms, climbing the wide staircases to rooms with hotplates on the third floor. (Religion was about the only thing my parents would have in common. She was a half-assed Catholic, and after lots of study, he became a half-assed Catholic, too.)

My mother had girlfriends—Eleanor, Dorothy, Beverly, a pair of Kays. They shopped together, ate in Child's or Schrafft's, "made" the Friday night novenas, and prayed for husbands. My father had boyfriends—Jackie, Bud, Marty, Mack. They drank beer together, rode motorcycles, shot pool.

Such a good-looking bunch of men, my mother said, so strange that none of these "gorgeous" men—all of whom, including my father, served their country—had any girls waiting for them.

With that conversational ball firmly in your lap, you drew your own conclusions. My mother was in the kitchen, filling the kettle for tea. One could only deduce that in her eagerness to be married and have a family, there were things about my father that my mother overlooked.

She was twenty-nine years old, still sleeping on the sheet-covered green damask sofa in her parents' Jackson Heights living room. Her parents had made her break up with Mr. Gordon,* her boss and the great love of her life, because he was older than she was and multi-divorced. Mom said that when she met my father, she was in a "dating dry spell." On Saturday nights she watched cops (which is pretty much how I spend *my* Saturday nights, come to think of it) dragging her drunken Aunt Nellie right past Mom's "bed" and into the "back bedroom," for which Aunt Nellie, since the spring of 1931, had paid ten dollars per week. As long as Aunt Nellie paid her room and board, nobody questioned her occasional overnight visitors, like the butt-naked man who once tumbled out of the closet in the middle of the night, landed at my grandmother's feet, and said, "I was just looking for a comb."

After my parents had been dating for a while (dates to which my father had actually worn blue suede shoes, back when Elvis was still driving trucks), my mother thought that at last her love had come along, but nobody told my father, because he disappeared. Never called when he said he would. Never came over when he promised. Mom said she spent the whole weekend staring at the phone. By Sunday afternoon, she'd had enough. She and my grandmother went to the

---

*pseudonym

movies. When they came home, there was a motorcycle parked in front of their ground-floor apartment. My mother said her heart stopped. But when they got inside, it wasn't my father but a "gorgeous" stranger sitting at the kitchen table, dead drunk and crying his eyes out with my grandfather's hand on his shoulder. "Marty here says his best friend is in love, and he's getting married, and leaving him forever," my grandfather said, looking at my mother over the tops of his tortoiseshell eyeglasses. My mother said that my grandfather, who had lost his three sons—one to meningitis, two to muscular dystrophy—looked as though he'd been crying, too. She described the scene as "surreal."

"Who is his friend in love with?" my mother asked, bewildered.

"You," my grandfather said.

Either this didn't strike my mother as odd, or she really wanted to get off that sofa.

Another story never told.

Because I had been a blond baby, my parents expected me to be blond. My hair was an unremarkable brown. They expected me to be short, like my mother. I was tall. They put cottage cheese and peaches in front of me, wanting me to be thin. I was not thin. They expected me to study tap dance like my mother, and who knows, maybe get on the *Ted Mack Amateur Hour*, but I had flat feet and needed something called a "cookie" in my little brown orthopedic shoes. Tap dance, like Keds sneakers, or anything remotely sportslike, was not for me. I was more like my friend Susan, who once said she'd gladly play tennis if someone else would chase the ball.

My parents thought that a talent scout might spot me in the Peanut Gallery of the *Howdy Doody Show*, and maybe I'd be the next *National Velvet*, but I got the chickenpox on the appointed day and that was the end of that.

My mother was thrilled with me when I was picked to be a Wise Man in the Christmas pageant. Even if you *do* have to wear a dishtowel over your head, she said, you never know who goes to these things. So while I waited to be discovered, I stood at the front of the stage, under the bright lights, next to pretty blond Margaret Moran,* the kneeling Blessed Mother. While Margaret stared lovingly at the vaguely naked, somewhat smelly Betsey-Wetsy doll that was wrapped in cotton batting and scary-looking in the manger, my eyes watered all over my cardboard box of myrrh.

My parents expected me to run around with the other kids on our street, instead of sitting on the steps of the apartment house reading Nancy Drew. They thought I'd play dolls with the other girls, not talk with the adults. At lunchtime, in the schoolyard, they thought I played tag with the others. They were surprised when the nuns told them that I sometimes disappeared. They wanted a carefree, bouncy kind of happy daughter, and not an underachiever filled with anxieties and fears, a worried daughter who spent recess sitting by herself in the back of the otherwise empty church, praying to God to relieve her of a quiet crushing sadness, a gruesome terror, all the symptoms of a bewildering depression that my mother tried to understand, but my child self had no words to describe. Two things saved me: one was a prayer card that I took with me everywhere, a picture of a soulful Jesus that said *YOU I need, YOU I want, YOU—I love you*, and the other was a small white diary that my mother somehow knew would help. Between the prayer card and the diary, I wrote myself free.

That was the first time writing saved me.

At the very least, my parents wanted a child who was normal, but what they got was a writer. (If you are from my

---

*pseudonym

Irish Catholic blue-collar background, saying that you wanted to be a writer was only a little less obnoxious than saying you wanted to be an aviatrix.)

"A WRITER?" someone would laugh. "Well, aren't YOU the bee's knees?" Then they'd go around calling you Keats or Yeats or even Here Comes the Great Authoress, when you've got nothing to show but desire. So you keep it all quiet, but the truth is that writers want to write so much that they are sometimes born holding crayons, a phenomenon not often remarked upon, nor completely understood, resulting in sweaty doctors leaving delivery rooms scribbled upon like Friendly's place mats.

(If you are thinking about the infant Mozart, born not holding a crayon but a quill—and this was long before epidurals, so nobody gives Mrs. Mozart enough credit—eager to shower, get into dry clothes, and have someone prop him up at the piano, well, think again.) As long as I can remember, I always wanted to write. To me—this tall, literal child with short, figurative goals—*writer* meant simply pressing pen to paper. Though my mother expected me to cure polio before that upstart Jonas Salk beat me to it, I wanted to work in the stationery aisle of Woolworth's on 82nd Street in Jackson Heights. I thought the hatchet-faced woman with the badly penciled reddish-brown eyebrows wouldn't be there forever. I was wrong again. She was there until Woolworth's closed, carried out feet first, clinging to the cotton candy machine.

I loved the things of writing, the heft of an old-fashioned fountain pen (like the one I use today); the somewhat salty, somewhat bloody smell of ink; the featherweight of a bright yellow pencil, my grandmother trying to sharpen mine with her paring knife, me leaning against her Ivory Snow–smelling "housedress," the pencil shavings sweetening the air, smelling like golden autumn leaves. I loved the words *typing paper*, *onionskin*, *loose-leaf*. I could think of nothing finer than spending my days in such delicious company. (Just the way I spend my life today, an irony not lost on me. And just like today, I can be home for lunch.)

To paraphrase what comic Paula Poundstone said of her job at IHOP, "It was a dream, but I'd make it happen."

Before I started school, my mother taught me to read. When the letters in my *Dick & Jane* primers suddenly made sense, a thrill shot through me. My mother brought me to the children's room of the Jackson Heights library, and then I wanted to be a librarian, for what could be better than being with books all day, reading whenever I wanted to. (Plus, I could go home for lunch.) The children's room at the library was a wonderland: all those books in shiny, crackling plastic covers that my fingers would stick to, the fingerprints of others there for me to see. The librarian who worked there was nice and also hugely fat, with not only breasts bursting out of her v-neck sweaters, but a thick patch of hair between them. Looking down her sweater was like one continuous "bring your ferret to work" day.

I loved the things of writing, I loved books and reading, but more than anything else, I loved stories. My grandfather, who wore a starched white shirt every day of his life, had a wealth of them. After dinner, whenever we ate together, he'd sit in the red brocade wing chair, and I'd sit at his feet, the scrap of "Oriental" carpeting beneath me a magic carpet carrying me back to old New York and all that he remembered: the horses; the gaslights; his (sanitized) eyewitness version of the Triangle Shirtwaist Factory fire.

Then he was suddenly gone, but my hunger for stories remained. I sat at my grandmother's kitchen table, watching Cousin Grace, a beer in her hand in the early afternoon. When she hugged me, the alcohol in her perfume and the alcohol on her breath made me cough. She was always in maternity dresses with "kangaroo" skirts, but she carried no baby, just a swollen liver. I watched Aunt Nellie—Uncle Nellie, some of the Irish relations called her—a woman in another time without a woman's currency (no husband, no children), and thought about her life. All she had was a back bedroom in someone else's apartment and a collection of hula dolls on her nightstand that I was forbidden to touch.

And I remember my father, standing at the bar in one gin mill after another, downing boilermakers more with a sense of grim duty than any hint of pleasure. Me, sent to find him and get him to come home. Going from the bright sunlight and pure air into darkness and cigarette smoke of the bar was one thing, but passing those bar stools was another: men and women turning around to reach for me, like in prison movies; me avoiding them, staring straight at my father's back, for he was the only one who never reached for me, never even turned around. What I have never had, and missed more than anything else in my life, was a father who'd protect me. If he asked Big John the bartender to get me a Shirley Temple, I was banished to a small table in the middle of the floor, prey to anyone passing by. I kept my head down and focused on the jagged scar on the back of my father's head, where he'd once fallen from the motorcycle. I told myself that Mr. Gordon (whom I imagined as a kindly, gray-haired man with glasses) was my real father, that any minute he'd show up and take me for ice cream.

I watched Lily Turner, our downstairs neighbor who wore purple hats long before anyone else and suffered from nervous breakdowns (whatever those were), taken over and over again to the hospital in a straitjacket. From my bedroom, I listened to my mother's friend Lucille in the kitchen, sobbing when her husband left her. Our Italian neighbor Josephine talked about the bombs falling on her Naples apartment house during

World War II, picking ceiling plaster out of the soup and serving it anyway.

What brought these women to this place and time? I wondered. But to me, every other story dissolved when our neighbor, K., was found murdered. In my novel, I turned her story into the story of a survivor, and I felt that somehow I'd given her another chance.

Half of me wanted to be a writer, but while I figured out how to go about it, the other half of me wanted to be Trixie Belden. Then I wanted to be Lois Lane, or Supergirl, but at least Lois carried a pad and a pen. Then I wanted to be the nameless, beautiful blond girl (it was probably a moonlighting Margaret Moran) on the Modess (*Modess rhymes with Oh, yes*) box. When an artist friend of my mother's said I looked like Kim Novak, I wanted to BE Kim Novak, but when I overheard someone say that her refrigerator was a better actress than Kim Novak, I wanted to be Audrey Hepburn in *The Nun's Story*, go to Africa as a missionary, and die for my faith.

"Oh, for Christ's sake," my mother said (yes, Mom, exactly), her head averted, trying to keep the long ash of her cigarette out of the stew. Saint Theresa of the Bloody Scourge she sometimes called me, dismantling my Blessed-Mother-in-a-Kleenex-tissue-box altars with frightening speed. She was walking me home from school one day when the sharp edge of my schoolbag's handle cut my palm. There was a surprising amount of blood. "Stigmata!" I cried, falling to my knees. My mother, who by then had smoking and slapping down to a science, pulled me to my feet. "No more holy bullshit!" she screamed, slapping the side of my head. (Why a self-proclaimed agnostic sends her children to Catholic school and then refers to all the Holy Day processions as "the goddamn nuns walking in circles" is anybody's guess. Another story never told.)

When I was in my early thirties, Patrick's wife and the mother of Patrick, who was healthy, and Jamie, who had inherited not only Mom's blue eyes but her family's Duchenne muscular dystrophy, I became a student. The reading and writing I'd done on my own was expansive. I hoped someday to write a book, but I thought I needed an English degree first. "An education is something no one can take from you," I heard my husband say to our older son, who was thinking of joining the Marines. Patrick Jr. listened, and so did I.

I'd been a hairnet-wearing chicken fryer in a bowling alley and found no fulfillment there. I'd been a pajama tagger at a local department store and in that I found no joy. (I didn't even get a new tagger—mine was secondhand with a dirty piece of tape on it that said TRACY R.) I was a cashier in the housewares department of Macy's, in the mall, where I had a panic attack during the one-day sale, left the cash register drawer agape, grabbed my purse, and, though it was the middle of winter, ran coatless through the parking lot and into my car. (If there's a purple maxi-coat still hanging in Macy's break room, it's mine.)

I was a typist in an investigative firm, where Denise from accounts payable kindly kept me updated on her husband's eighty-four-year-old stepfather's condition on life support, when all I wanted to do was to eat cheese crackers from the vending machine and stuff her frosted head into the dirty microwave.

I looked at Jamie, getting worse and worse, and in the dawn hours poured all of my thoughts into the journals, wrote myself through it. That was the second time writing saved me.

One day, into the tenth year of my two-year community college career, I was walking through a hallway near the teachers' lounge and saw an ad for a writer's conference. I applied and, to my shock, was accepted. Our assignment was to write one chapter of a novel and—I know this sounds all Lana Turner/Schwab's Drugstore-ish, but it's true—the instructor, a novelist herself, told me to send the chapter to a young agent she knew in New York. (Just my luck: when I was finally discovered, Ted Mack was dead.)

On a hot summer day, the agent called. My then-long hair was in rollers, mostly to keep the hair off my neck. Our 1990 cordless phone, big as a brick, had a long antenna, which had to be fully extended to hear anything. "Tell me about yourself," the young agent said, and at that exact moment Jamie rolled up to me in his wheelchair and asked for a pencil. Most of the time, with Jamie, I tried to be Mother Theresa and do small things for him with great love (and sometimes, loud screaming), but that day I wanted to kill him. I went out on the back deck, where the clothesline was. Somehow or other, the phone's antenna went through my hair rollers, and I got caught up in the wet laundry hanging from the line. I told the young agent all about myself—what I wanted to say, really, was that I spent a lot of my time in the supermarket, or Cheap John's, which was pretty much my life then—but I left out the part about the jockey shorts dripping on my face.

And that's how the glittering world of publishing opened up for me.

My novel took two years to write. *Rubato* is the musical term William Carlos Williams used when asked how he combined medicine and poetry. "I steal a little from here," he said, "and a little from there." Rubato was how I wrote that novel, threading it through Jamie's pneumonias, recoveries, doctor's visits, waiting rooms, recovery rooms, examination rooms, school vacations, the trip to Disneyworld (although the boys were eighteen and sixteen), before Jamie's spinal operation that three out of four doctors doubted he'd survive. I wrote the novel through the care-filled days and the sleepless nights, once falling asleep sitting on the windowsill at Blockbuster, waiting for Jamie to pick out a movie.

I wrote the novel around the calls I got from the high school nurse, when Jamie needed to use the bathroom. Everyone in the nurse's office, and Jamie's school aide, seemed appalled when I arrived and threw my purse and car keys on the floor in a red-faced fury. (It's not HIM, I told myself, it's his CONDITION, but who else to be angry at, other than me?) The lifting and the wiping—seventeen years old, and this was his life—then getting him back into the wheelchair, almost threw me on the floor with both compassion and self-hatred. When I kissed Jamie's head, the school nurse and the aide looked at me through cold eyes. I got back into the huge van I had to learn to drive, collapsed in tears, drove home . . . and worked on the novel.

That was the third time writing saved me.

But the thing about writing is that it saves not just a few times, but over and over again.

In my journals, after Jamie died, I wrote my way out of the biggest, blackest sorrow of my life. (Even in the dark, writing saved me.) Oh, Jamie. Then I wrote a memoir and discovered that writing and publishing are two different things. If writing about our family's illness (for not only had Jamie inherited muscular dystrophy, but so had my nephews, Chris and Jason) felt like I was rolling the stone from my tomb, publishing it felt like I was forced to go back in. I gave one reading after another, stood at one podium after another, told one incredulous audience after another that of those four laughing little boys on my book's cover, only my son Patrick was healthy. "Which boy did you lose?" a smiling, middle-aged woman in glasses once asked me. Smiling back, I pointed to Jamie, the happy toddler on the right. At that moment, publishing almost killed me. I needed years to recover from the experience, but I did, and now I'm back.

Writing is what I love: writing is my life's work.

In literature as in love, said Sir Walter Scott, courage is half the battle.

CHRISTINE KEHL O'HAGAN is the author of *Benediction at the Savoia*, a novel, and the memoir *The Book of Kehls*. Both books received starred Kirkus Reviews, the latter a Kirkus "Best Book of 2005" selection. Her essays have appeared in *Between Friends*, *The Day My Father Died*, *Lives through Literature*, *Facts on File: The American Novel*, and *For Keeps*. She received the Jerry Lewis Writing Award and has contributed to the *New York Times*, *Newsday*, and several Long Island publications. O'Hagan is currently working on a second memoir, *Commencing to Forget*. Her Web site is http://www .christinekehlohagan.com.

JAMES BRYLONSKI

WATERCOLORS

Sandra Gulland

1962

I was in my last year at Berkeley High School in Berkeley, California. There were over six hundred of us in the graduating class that spring. Crooners sang in the hallways at lunchtime. We could Watusi, we were crazy for the Stroll, we'd been Twisting for years.

But it wasn't always party time. We were likely the only high school in the United States to protest and succeed in banning assemblies sponsored by the military. In English, I sat next to Tracy Simms, founder of Students for Equality (which I joined), and leader the following year of the first—the *very* first—sit-in, to take place in San Francisco at the Sheraton Palace Hotel, protesting their racist hiring policies. (As a result, the Sheraton Palace Hotel hired their first black employee.)

The high school was close to the University of California at Berkeley. I was excused from class to go hear Bobby Kennedy. Walking across campus toward our home in the hills, I saw tall, storklike Aldous Huxley leaning into a wind. *Brave New Word* indeed. The times they *were* a-changin'.

These were years of ferment, important beginnings. Battles had been pitched in the South—and won. A just society was more than a dream; youth would make it happen; we were living it. A year earlier, John Kennedy had been elected president. His words "Ask not what your country can do for you, ask what you can do for your country" were displayed on bus posters. The year following 1962 saw our dreams crushed with the assassination of JFK. Years of violence followed as our brothers and lovers and friends were forced to fight in a war they opposed.

Two times in the spring of 1968, suffering insomnia, I turned on the television late in the night to news of yet another assassination: April 4, Martin Luther King; June 6, Bobby Kennedy. I'd been campaigning for Bobby Kennedy that afternoon. The next day, sitting on a sand dune overlooking Half Moon Bay, I made the decision to leave the United States, the country of my birth. It was a hard decision born out of violence. The inevitable logic of my convictions meant that I would have to join in violent protest. There seemed to be no other path and, as a Quaker-attender, it was not a path I was willing to take. I looked for a more peaceful land in which to build a nest. It took years (emigrating is complex), but I persevered and found that peace in Canada.

But 1962 was before all that—before the draft, before bad acid trips, before Charles Manson, Altamont, and the shocking waves of assassinations. In '62, everything seemed possible.

I was seventeen and a passionate painter. I'd converted half of my bedroom into a studio and worked on huge five-by-three-foot canvases, stretched and sized with the rabbit-skin glue I cooked up in the family kitchen. I made pigment, too, to save money. Oils were expensive, especially given the way I loved to slather on the colors with a palette knife. In a step toward self-sufficiency, I'd been given a clothing allowance of $25 a month, but most of it was furtively spent on art supplies.

I remember one lovely spring day, walking up into the Berkeley hills, toward home, with my wood stretcher bars balanced on my shoulders, a length of folded canvas under my arm. I was humming. I felt energized, excited: I was carrying the promise of a painting. I couldn't wait to fit the frame together, stretch the canvas, slather on the rabbit-skin glue. I had paint under my nails and paint splotched on my skirt. "Are you a painter?" a boy asked at a bus stop. "Yes," I said. "I *am*."

My best friend was Tamar Etingen, also an artist. (And still an artist.) We were radicals and proud of it. We weren't Beatniks—we were too young for that—but we often looked the part. We were serious, independent, scornful of the cliques. Walking up to Shattuck Avenue during lunch break, we bemoaned our maturity, in fact, fearful that an airhead childishness would overtake us later in life, convinced that mindless frivolity was a stage that could not be avoided. (This may well be true.)

After our last day of high school, Tamar and I were on a bus: I don't recall why we were on the bus together, or where we were going. What I do recall is that we were on Berkeley's south side, not far from the university campus. The bus pulled to a stop. An old woman—short and plump with frizzy white hair—stepped on, calling out to a friend who was already seated, "Mable, I got the watercolors!"

It was her excitement and passion that struck me. I turned to Tamar and said, "I want to be like her when I'm old."

Now, well into my sixties, I'm still not what most of *my* generation would call "old"—although, in truth, I'm beginning to see it in my face and feel it in my bones. And so how do I measure up? Am I that woman getting on the bus?

Tamar and I invented a religion we called Spushism. It had more to do with the miracle of creativity than spiritualism. The creative urge was a tsunami wave in our lives, as powerful as—and possibly powerfully linked to—hormones. I was, if anything, too charged, too scattered as a youth to make anything concrete of my creative energy. It wasn't until middle age that I found the steady focus to harness it.

My parents—my mother, especially—were supportive. She chose to ignore that my clothing allowance was going for my art. She argued with her brother, who scowlingly insisted that *all* of the head of a portrait must be within the frame of the painting. I ignored him, secretly pleased that my work was worthy of heated adult debate.

Why did I stop painting? Against my parents' wishes—especially those of my mother—I married very young, not yet even twenty. He was a painter, and we shared a storefront studio on Potrero Hill in San Francisco. Before long, I was no longer a painter but a painter's wife. I put away my oils, brushes, and palette knives, and in my sleepless nights I would write—words of confusion, longing, and misery.

For the first two and a half years of university life, at San Francisco State, I majored in mathematics on the assumption that I would get more out of my education if it was in a subject that was entirely foreign to me. In truth, I loved the logic of it, the locked-down stunning simplicity of the equal sign, the pleasure of puzzling out formulas. In chaotic times, I found the purity of mathematics psychologically soothing.

However, in my third year, at the University of California at Berkeley, I quickly learned that pleasure in math was not nearly enough: one had to breathe and sleep it. I was in way out of my depth. I sat on a stone bench on campus thinking about what my major should be, now that I had to give up math. My second choice was comparative literature—the study of which I still long for!—but a quick glance at the language requirements made it clear that I would be in school for the rest of my life. The study of English literature came naturally to me. My mother had showered me with books throughout my teens. One Christmas I got stacks and stacks (books were the only thing I wanted): Thomas Hardy, Charles Dickens, William Blake, Virginia Woolf, James Joyce. Hungrily, I had consumed these works. The study of English literature was the natural choice, and so, with resignation, I switched.

In 1968, my then husband was accepted to the Art Institute in Chicago. On short notice, Roosevelt University accepted me for the final year of my BA. After prestigious Berkeley, I saw Roosevelt University as a ramshackle school, a place where anyone could go. After all, they had accepted *me*. It was, in fact, a good university. The classes were small (unlike at Berkeley), the study much more intimate, the teachers ardent academics with one foot at the University of Chicago and one at Roosevelt.

I remember two classes especially: one on Shakespeare, and one on Henry James, both excellent. As long ago as this was—

forty years?—I remember working on papers for both, long into the night. "Masterful," my Shakespeare teacher said breathlessly in response to my essay on *Richard II*. I was stunned.

One morning I was in the administration office. On the floor below, the Black Panthers were having a noisy gathering. A black student handed me the papers I was seeking and we talked about the meeting downstairs. He had withdrawn his support for the Black Panthers, he told me, because of the way they treated women. "There can be no equality without equality for women," he said. Outside the private grumblings of the women in my family, this was the first formal statement in support of equality for women I'd heard.

I worked part-time in the accounting office, in charge of the student loans. I'm a careful person, systematic and conscientious, but somehow I'd made a mess of it. Perhaps my problems resulted from the lack of supervision, for soon there was a new boss. I remember his shock, looking over his office staff, seeing me in the corner puzzling over my boxes of index cards (no computers), in long blond braids and smoking a little pipe (I was trying to quit smoking cigarettes). This was me at twenty-something—and I like to imagine that it might be me at ninety-something, too, were it not for fact that I have, finally, truly given up smoking and that now it would take decades for my thinning hair to grow sufficiently long.

I was writing poetry then. On impulse, I submitted and won first prize for a poem titled "Brain." I have no recollection of this poem, but what I do remember very clearly is the uncomfortable awards ceremony, the handful of people seated in a little room high up in the old university building, the rambling and incoherent poet recruited to give out the award certificates weaving behind the podium, grasping it with white-knuckled hands, his "agent" or "handler" or "sister" (for all I knew) having urgent, hushed words with him at the window during a break. I had the impression that she was persuading him not to jump. In fact, I think he tried. Such was my introduction to the writing life.

In the year after my husband and I separated, I was published for the first time, an article in a popular national Canadian newsweekly. That night, I went on a painfully awkward blind date with another couple. Over dinner, the young woman began talking about the article she'd read that morning, written by a woman who had spent a year in the Arctic. As she excitedly recounted the details, I was too shy to reveal that I was the author.

My second husband, Richard, introduced me as a writer to his Canadian family. This startled me; I was working as an editor at that time. Later, after our first baby, sitting in the Peasant's Larder restaurant in Cabbagetown, Toronto, I told him that I wanted to write a novel. He was not surprised.

We moved north shortly after, to the country. There, I began setting my alarm for 5:00, rising an hour before our two children awoke in order to "free-write." After a year, I read these pages, looking for the kernels of a story—only to discover that what I had were hundreds of pages, all on the subject of exhaustion.

It took time. Life was both demanding and diverting. I kept telling myself that I was going to write that novel "some day." Turning forty, I was reading a silly inspirational book that suggested one imagine the words on one's tombstone. My tombstone came immediately into view, etched with the words: *She never got around to it.* If I was going to write, I had to begin.

The following summer, on a visit to see my family in Berkeley, I had yet another run-in with yet another grumpy uncle. I'd returned from a shopping trip to San Francisco with three books on writing. (One I bought for its title alone: *You*

Can Write a Novel!) "I want to write a novel," I told him. We were sitting on the back porch of my parents' home, watching as my younger cousins played. He scoffed and said, with derision, "You can't learn how to write from *books*." I was happy that he lived to see at least one of my novels published. (With respect to his memory—I did like this uncle—I'll suppress a childish raspberry.)

At a party one night with friends, nearing midnight—the children asleep at last—we decided to each declare what it was we wished to accomplish before the age of fifty. All I wanted, I said, was to publish one novel: *one* book, with my name on the spine.

I didn't quite make it. My first novel was published in the spring of 1995, four months after my fiftieth birthday. The moment I put that book on the shelf—to see what it would look like set between *The Tin Drum* by Günter Grass and *Charades* by Janette Turner Hospital (my first writing teacher)—I wanted more: I wanted to see an entire shelf of books with my name on the spines.

Now, fourteen years later, I do have a shelf of books, books in many languages, books with my name on the spines. I will not deny that this gives me great (*great*) pleasure. But writing is a vocation that is constantly challenging. I think of the life story told by an early instructor. In everything he'd ever attempted, he'd succeeded. He'd had a breakdown, it was so boring. His therapist suggested he become a writer: "Then you will never feel that you've succeeded." How true! I'm reading Haruki Murakami's memoir *What I Talk about When I Talk about Running*, and this line jumps out: "What's crucial is whether your writing attains the standards you've set for yourself." Unfortunately (or not), those standards are a moving target: with each book, the bar is raised.

And what about that deeper thing: that *passion* for creativity? I'm wearier now; I've less spark, less energy. Where are the bright flares of inspiration going off like fireworks in a night sky? Where are the ideas that come in a rush, send me scrambling for a scrap of paper? The tsunami is more of a placid river . . . or, some days, a swamp. Yet I know that swamp well: it is rich with hidden ferment. The swamp is where novels begin.

We become our parent. How can it be otherwise? I look at the age spots on my hands in dismay, the blue veins, the dry, wrinkled skin, a skeletal outline emerging. I remember looking with disgust at my mother's hands, and now those hands are my own. I note with surprise words used to describe me of late. "Birdlike," my chiropractor said of my bones. "Like eggshells," the manicurist said of my nails. I seem to have become fragile, frail—like my mother in her declining years. I'm thinking of her more kindly now as I follow her path. She went here before me.

I remember her longing for an interest. She'd been a painter, a potter, a quilter. She was curious, creative by nature and had had periods of passionate interest in one craft or another, one subject or another. Stirring a pot at the kitchen stove, she would lose herself staring at a painting, trying to puzzle it out. For a period of time in my youth, a microscope sat on the counter beside the refrigerator, which was home to the molds and "cultures" she was studying. Her latest interest, rather surprisingly, had been in the economy, investments, the ebb and flow of money. But that subject no longer intrigued her, and there was nothing to take its place. She no longer felt curious; nothing called to her. I imagine she felt adrift, without a rudder. In truth, she was ailing; she'd begun—without any of us knowing—that long, slow descent toward death. First, her energy ebbed, then her strength. At the last, cruelly, she lost the ability to read, to think.

Turning sixty, sixty-one, sixty-two, sixty-three—none of these fazed me—but sometimes, now, at sixty-four, I begin to feel "my age," begin to have spells where my hands cramp, periods of feeling feeble, stooped, my wits hay-wired. Where is the woman who pulls fancy from clouds, who walks dreamlike into distant worlds?

Yet I know the remedy: *creativity*. I am, in this moment, between novels, and without something creative brewing, I begin to pale. In my early forties, a homeopathic doctor examined the irises of my eyes and said, "The problem is that you are not using your creativity." I smiled wanly and showed him the book I had with me, one of the many I was acquiring on how to write.

But how to begin, yet again? Resistance, I remind myself, is the first stage. I set daily goals—sketch out scenes; exercise; meditate; research—and daily I flounder, my energy and time scattered over an unmanageable To Do list.

I failed Self-Control in grade three. *Failed!* My mother found it amusing. I remember staring incredulously at that little white card, the black lines in a grid, the damning mark. I didn't even know what Self-Control was.

It *is* a confusing bit of business, certainly. Some things must not be overly controlled (feelings, for example). Other things require a watchful measure (cheesecake, Southern Comfort). Aging requires quite a bit of surveillance, I'm discovering: of weight, pills, exercise, sleep. I monitor my body with all the attention I give my equally aging car, attentive to any aches and pains.

My mother died "on my watch." My sister, her partner, and I had decided to take turns sitting with her through the long night—her last, we feared. She'd been in a somewhat peaceful, semiconscious state for days, but that evening her breathing had become markedly labored. My sister woke me at midnight. I was sleeping in my mother's bed—she was downstairs on a hospital bed set up in the living room, attended by a nurse aide.

I hadn't had much sleep and I wondered how I would stay alert. I thought of the volume of poetry I'd noticed on my mother's bedside table, an anthology of American poetry. I ran upstairs and grabbed it, then settled back down in the worn armchair close to the hospital bed. The nurse aide sat anxiously by the medications that had been set on the woven Japanese cloth covering an antique Tansu. The lights of San Francisco could be seen through the wood Venetian blinds. All around this lovely room were the pots, baskets, and art objects my mother loved.

I opened the anthology and glanced through the pages. Some of the poems were starred—these were the ones she had loved. In the margins were her notes in a careful hand. The book had obviously been with her for decades. I was surprised that it was beside her bed even now, for she had been unable to read for some time. Leafing through the pages, seeing her youthful hand in the margins, I realized how much poetry had been a part of her life. I recalled coming home from grade school to find her with her feet propped up on the kitchen table, absorbed in a book of poetry. One year she took an old paperback edition of Robert Frost's poetry to read on a trip to Europe. (No light reading for her.) The yellowed pages scattered before boarding. I love to think of my mother and father frantically scrambling to gather up the words of Robert Frost as the last call for boarding was announced.

The hospice nurse had told us that hearing was the last sense to go, and that the dying can hear your words, even if they seem to be unconscious. And so I decided that I would read poetry to my mother. I thought it fitting that in what could well be her last hours, she would hear words she loved, words that were beautifully familiar to her.

I leafed through the volume, looking for suitable poems. e. e. cummings, Theodore Roethke, William Carlos Williams, Wallace Stevens, Robert Frost—I'd come to know and love these poets through my mother. In the second year of university, I'd worked part-time as night-shift elevator operator at the Mark Hopkins Hotel in San Francisco and idled the long hours by memorizing Roethke's "The Waking."

I wake to sleep.

I began to read, stopping now and then, frozen with the realization that my mother's breathing had stopped. The nurse aide and I watched, silently counting out the seconds, then exhaled with relief when yet another breath came.

The university Campanile rang one bell. I resumed reading. It was on the last line of Edna Saint Vincent Millay's "Wild Swans" that I looked up to see my mother gently struggling for breath like a fish out of water—once, twice—and then no more.

Later, much later—after my father's cries of anguish, after the morticians had come for my mother's body, after the moving memorial, the sorting and adjusting, the painful putting away—I remembered that my mother had pointed out this particular poem to me long ago. I was in my twenties. We were standing in the sunny kitchen, the windows opening onto a view of San Francisco Bay, a wood bowl of oranges set on the kitchen table. "It's about death," she told me. "Isn't it lovely?"

How miraculously fitting that she should die to those words.

Who was it who said that living is about learning how to die? My mother lived and died in poetry, and that's a wonderful thing. She had great stretches of desert in her life, but she nurtured herself with creativity—with painting (for which she had a talent), with clay, with fabric, with words. I begin to see that in my own arid, counting times (counting pennies, vitamins, leg lifts, calories) I'm missing the main event. I need to enliven my weary heart. I need poetry in my life. I *need* to write, and perhaps I even need to paint again.

My relationship with my mother was often conflicted. She had high aesthetic standards, and I felt I could never measure up. If I wasn't published in the *New Yorker*, I could not be considered a *true* writer—at least this was my harsh perception of her judgment of me. And yet, of course, when I did publish, she was my proudest fan. "You're Sandra Gulland's mother?" a bookstore clerk had asked her, in wonder, to which she beamed: "I *am*."

And yes, she *is*. A writer's life is one of constant doubt, the struggle neverending. I think at such times of my mother and gain courage from that: I am doing what she wanted me to do, I am being who she wanted me to be—and I am grateful for that.

And yes: I got the watercolors.

SANDRA GULLAND is the author of the Josephine B. trilogy: *The Many Lives & Secret Sorrows of Josephine B.*; *Tales of Passion, Tales of Woe*; and *The Last Great Dance on Earth*.

This collection has sold over a million copies worldwide and has been published in thirteen languages. Her latest novel, *Mistress of the Sun*, was published in the spring of 2008 and immediately became a best seller. Her Web site is http://www.sandragulland.com.

THROUGH THE LOOKING GLASS

Aviva Layton

When I was a child in Sydney, I used to spend hours staring into the three-paneled mirror on my mother's dressing table. Her pale orange Yardley's powder box— I can see it as clearly as if it were before me now—was embossed with fluffy white puffs. Beside it was a crystal tray containing a tortoiseshell brush and comb. I never saw her pick up any of these things, let alone use them.

Whenever my parents were away I'd go into their room, sit down on the faded brocade stool, and stare into the mirror. I was only

131

interested in the two moveable side panels. I would arrange them endlessly, swiveling the two sections back and forth so that my image was reflected over and over again, each one identical yet each one somehow tantalizingly different. I was haunted by the sense that, despite the myriad of reflected images, there was no real me, only a series of fragments. The more I stared, the less I saw, but however queasy it made me feel, something kept me going back, as if I expected some transformative moment that would enable me to discover that elusive entity, my true self.

That I was never able to find it only heightened my suspicions that I was a changeling child, always fated to be an outsider. While other children loved reading *Sleeping Beauty* or *Little Red Riding Hood* or *Cinderella*, the Grimms' tale that haunted me most was *The Strange Feast*, a bizarre and grotesque story in which the main characters were two sausages—a blood sausage and a liver sausage. The blood sausage invited the liver sausage to come to her house for a meal. As the liver sausage was about to enter the house, she heard a voice warning her that she was approaching a murderous trap. She ran for her life and, looking back, saw the blood sausage leaning out of the attic window brandishing a long sharp knife and crying out, "If I had caught you, I would have had you." Like that liver sausage, a voice inside me whispered that I, too, was caught in some awful trap and that if I didn't get out as soon as possible, I'd be destroyed.

Not all my thoughts were so nightmarish. I also daydreamed about what I would like to be when I grew up, but even then I knew they were unattainable fantasies. I would become an opera singer (I'd been passed over for the coveted part of Yum-Yum in my school's annual production of *The Mikado*); a ballerina (I'd been ignominiously expelled from Madame Olga's ballet classes); a world-famous violinist (I took violin lessons but hated them); an actress (I was so petrified with stage fright, I forgot all my lines when acting Puck in my drama club).

These daydreams, however, were rare. It always made me feel uneasy that so many of my school friends had such precise plans for their futures—they would go to college for a couple of years, meet their future husbands there, marry, have children. Even before I hit adolescence, those plans filled me with dread. I thought much more intensely about what I *didn't* want to be and, above all, I didn't want to be the dutiful Jewish daughter of immigrant parents who were never able to reconcile themselves to the fact that they lived at the far end of the world. Unlike them, I would escape Australia and, unlike my mother, whose answer to any request of mine was an automatic "No," I would live my life responding to everything with a loud "Yes."

Most of all, I definitely did not want to be someone whose name was Aviva. In 1930s Sydney, one of the most popular names was Gloria, and I desperately wanted to experience the glory of being a Gloria instead of an Aviva, whose very name shouted *outsider*. As one of my teachers pointed out, it was a palindrome, which meant it was spelled the same way backwards as forwards. Instead of being proud of the distinction, I felt it was an apt symbol for what I felt about myself—I was someone whose beginning and end were interchangeable. I scrawled the name *Gloria* inside my books. Wrote it on the inside of my schoolbag. Whispered it to myself before I went to sleep at night. Gloria. Now that was a name to be proud of, a name that didn't need any explanation, that went with Shirley Temple curls, embroidered aprons, and parents who didn't speak Yiddish loudly in public. Who didn't speak Yiddish at all, in fact, because they were nice, polite Australian Christians. And I didn't want to be the only one in my classroom whose father wasn't fighting on the front line, defending Australia against The Yellow Peril. I so intensely wanted him to wear the iconic brown slouch hat of the Australian Infantry Corps that I envied those classmates whose fathers had either been killed or were missing in action; these were the heroes whose actions conferred heroism on their children. As for me, I felt only shame when I walked in the street with my parents, trying my best to fall behind so no one would associate me with these awkward foreigners who didn't seem to be aware either of their embarrassed daughter or their guttural accents.

But above all, I wanted my parents to be in love. Sadly mismatched, they lived parallel lives, coming together only to quarrel bitterly. While my mother craved the glamorous life—parties, dancing, dressing fashionably—my father was a sad failure of a man who struggled unsuccessfully in the rag trade and who read Spinoza and Maimonides in his spare time. I felt stifled by the miasma of unhappiness that permeated our small flat and knew from an early age that my parents felt trapped, and that whatever love they once had for each other had long since turned to deep resentment. I don't remember a single loving gesture between them, a hug, a kiss, a tender touch. Therapists have described how traumatized a child can become by accidentally witnessing their parents in the throes of lovemaking.

My childhood trauma was that I never did.

I muddled through primary and high school, always just scraping by, always deeply confused about who I was, what my desires or abilities—if any—might be. All I knew is that I felt unsettlingly different, but it was a difference that didn't make me feel superior or more interesting to those around me.

On the contrary, it heightened my sense of unease. It was only when I finally entered university that I found some sort of escape from my confusions. Not knowing what I wanted to study, I enrolled in a general arts course but quickly found that my main interest was in a group that called itself The Push and was composed of intellectuals, Bohemians, free thinkers, libertarians. They drank, they fucked, they said things like "every act of copulation is a conscious act of opposition to the state." They read Bertrand Russell, Havelock Ellis, and smuggled banned copies of *The Tropic of Cancer* and *Lady Chatterley's Lover* into literature classes. I soon lost my much-despised virginity and threw myself into a world of books. Books showed me for the first time in my life that there was a world beyond the one in which I'd always been an alien. I felt relieved and vindicated, but something stopped me from leaving home and throwing in my lot with this group: a troubling and nagging inner voice that told me that I didn't really belong there either. I clung to the idea that somewhere in the large world I could finally feel at home, that somewhere I would meet a wonderful man who would make me whole.

Finally, in 1955, at the age of twenty-one, with a minimum of carefully saved money, I left both home and country. My preferred destination was New York, but it was impossible to get a work visa. I chose Montreal, where I arrived with the equivalent of five Australian pounds and not a clue as to what I was going to do next. I was scared but elated. I had escaped!

The irony was that shortly after I'd found work in a bookstore, I happened to meet a man who was Jewish, but who was the antithesis of any Jew I've ever met in Australia. Irving Layton was a poet who was two decades older than I, brilliant and compelling, someone who knew exactly what he was des-tined to do: write poetry. One look at him and, like Alice, I stepped through the tantalizing watery scrim of the looking glass into another world, one in which I could banish all those doubts about my own identity. Like Olenka, the troubled character in Chekhov's short story "The Darling," who dis-appeared into whomever her husband or lover at the time happened to be, I disappeared into Irving.

Mirrors had always betrayed me, but looking into the mirror of Irving's eyes I saw for the first time a reflection that had definition, one that was more me than I was myself. He was writing me; he was me writing. Along with that revelation came the inevitable fear that if he looked away for even one second, I would disappear. And he looked away often. There were women, legions of them, and they induced in me the sort of clawing jealousy that only someone with a tenuous sense of self can experience. There were many times when I pretended both to myself and to Irving that I was going to leave, but underneath it all I knew I never would.

Ten troubled years into our relationship, I gave birth to our son, David, and the whole focus of my life changed. The first time I held him in my arms, I made a vow never to burden him with the same anomie I had experienced as a child, never to stifle him. I would be a brilliant mother. More than a mother—a friend, an enabler, a constant yes-sayer—and it was only with the greatest reluctance that I agreed to return to Sydney when he was only a few weeks old. My father had died some months before, and my mother wanted to see not only her grandson but also her daughter. I remember having serious misgivings as I sat on that Qantas flight, staring out the tiny window, my infant son in my lap and the Pacific spread out below, trying to make a con-nection between the life I had been living since leaving Australia and the reality of flying toward my past.

At first I was intoxicated by the incredible beauty of Sydney—the intensity of light, the jungle of gardenias, jasmine, frangipanis, the hypnotic thrum of the cicadas, the dazzling shimmer of the harbor. Why on earth had I ever wanted to leave? Why on earth had I been so unhappy? But before long my misgivings were justified. Despite the presence of my baby, within twenty-four hours of arriving I felt as if I'd never left. My mother was still living in the Bellevue Hill flat, that same miasma of unhappiness still permeating the atmosphere. And there was that three-piece mirror, now a little speckled, the faded orange powder box, the still unused tortoiseshell comb and brush. Nothing had changed. I avoided looking into the mirror in case my fragmented images were still there, waiting to jump out at me from their glassy prison.

Returning to Sydney after a ten-year absence was like being measured for one's height on the marked inches of a familiar doorpost. How much had I grown? Or maybe I'd shrunk. Because I hadn't lived my adult life here, my childhood memories had been frozen in time and, to my surprise, I often felt an intense and stabbing connection to the country of my birth. Each corner had its own particular resonance, each sound its haunting echo, and I realized that being born in a place—any place—ties you to it for life. It wasn't abstract patriotism I felt, but a longing for the primal imprint of the sights and sounds and smells of my childhood, however troubling they might have been.

One day, I decided to visit the old row house in Paddington where we had lived before moving to Bellevue Hill. Despite gentrification, the now trendy and expensive houses still felt like the leaky old tenements they had been when we lived there. As I paused before our old house, now brick-washed and spiffed up almost beyond recognition, I caught a familiar dank whiff coming off the walls and felt as if I'd been sucked into a psychic wormhole, never to emerge on the other side, if indeed the other side even existed.

To compound my sense of time-traveling backwards, one of my friends insisted on taking me to the Hyde Park Barracks, which had been turned into a museum. "Close your eyes," she whispered, as we rounded a corner. When I was told to open them, I gasped. There in front of us was a perfect reproduction of a booth of Repins, our old university coffeeshop haunt where we took turns either drinking coffee or serving it. Chained to the table like a sacred text was a tattered menu and to one side, in a glass cabinet, a cream bowl, coffeepot, sugar tongs, and a faded waitress uniform. It could very well have been the one I'd worn. As we moved through the rooms, I saw the familiar objects I'd grown up with—tray-mobiles, beaded milk-jug covers, ice boxes, teapot cozies—all of them locked up behind glass as if they were historical artifacts. I had the spooky feeling that if I stayed much longer, someone would lock me up behind glass, too.

On my last day, I took a farewell walk through the Botanical Gardens and experienced a similar time-tilt. I came across a bandstand with khaki-clad soldiers playing the popular Second World War song "A Brown Slouch Hat." Women in '40s floral frocks strolled around the bandstand, absurd little hats perched like birds' nests on top of their permed hair. I was mesmerized, until an officious young woman waved me away, and I realized I'd wandered onto a movie set.

For the rest of my trip, I felt inundated by tidal waves of emotion—feelings of being completely at home and yet being utterly alien. The alienated feelings dominated, and when I looked out of the plane window at the receding outline of the Sydney Harbour Bridge, I vowed never to return before at least another decade had passed.

I traveled extensively before those ten years were up. Morocco. England. Ireland. France. Portugal. Italy. India. Indonesia. Nepal. Israel. Thailand. Turkey. The '60s had vindicated those of us who had felt like outsiders and, to that end, we traveled all over the world, dragging our hapless children in our wake. Too obsessed with our own lives, we blinded ourselves to the fact that children crave stability in order to counterbalance the anarchy and chaos of childhood. What so many of us turned into—certainly, I did—were parents who decided to be children, thus forcing our children to become parents. I'm not denying the liberating value of the '60s—they had a profound and positive effect on the world we find ourselves in now—but for many of our sons and daughters, those years were toxic. I have friends whose children have disappeared into the void, others whose children refuse to speak to them, a good number who have become drug addicts, committed suicide, who suffer from a variety of psychic ailments.

I remember both Irving and myself insisting on staying at the cheapest hotels in order to experience the "authentic" India, completely disregarding the fact that what was authentic for us was nightmarish for our son. "Adventures" we called them, and to this day the word evokes shudders in David. There's one incident from that period that I'll never forget, nor will he. We were traveling through the Atlas Mountains of Morocco and stayed briefly at a hashish farm that, apart from the locals who actually harvested the crop, was full of expatriate dropouts. There was one American family we'd noticed whose son, like ours, was eleven. We'd seen him earlier in the day walking along a dusty path, and David had been relieved to find another child. We saw him again that night, sitting cross-legged on a tattered carpet, taking turns with his parents smoking a chillum, which was almost as large as he was. His eyes were hollow and empty. The two boys stared across the room at each other, and I shuddered to realize that it could have been my own son looking out at the world with those lost eyes.

The most fateful journey took place in the Greek village of Molyvos on the island of Lesbos. All three of us—Irving, David, and myself—had fallen in love with the place ever since we'd discovered it in 1965 and, since we both taught—Irving was a university professor, I was a lecturer—we were able to visit for three months every summer. It was here where Irving and I were happiest with each other, but also here, ironically, where our relationship ended. I could put the blame for the collapse of our marriage on his solipsism or on his compulsive need to womanize, but that would not only be cowardly but false. Whatever it was that he needed from me, I needed more from him and it was a need that, like a sieve, could never be filled. I'd wrapped my life around a powerful man and tied the package so tightly that I couldn't unfasten the knot even if I had wanted to and, for nearly twenty years, I had not.

That I was finally able to leave Irving was an event I've never been able to explain fully, not even to myself. One summer I met another man, Leon Whiteson, a writer from London who was living in Molyvos, and I was instantly attracted. At first, it was going to be yet another affair, the latest in a string of lovers I'd accumulated over the years in order to keep up with Irving's ladies. However, like so many other events in my life, it spun out of control, and what followed was an incredibly painful period for everyone. Leon returned to London and, by the time Irving and I returned to Toronto, it was agreed that he would move out. For nearly a year, I yo-yoed between the two cities. I would have gone on like that for as long as I could get away with it had Leon not insisted that the merry-go-round be stopped and that David and I move to London. It was yet another wrench for David, made easier by the fact that, while Irving undeniably loved him, he was essentially a stranger to his own son, a patriarch rather than a father.

Because I had never learned to differentiate the boundaries between Irving and myself, I experienced intense feelings of panic. Who could I possibly be if I weren't him? The focus of Irving's life was poetry; the focus of Leon's life was me and, perversely, it made me feel uncomfortable. Selling our house in Toronto, uprooting thirteen-year-old David from his friends— yet another "adventure"—and moving to a dismal London flat in order to be with Leon turned out to be a necessary, though painful, jolt. It took me a long time to learn how to accept the feeling of being equal, of realizing that what I did or said was more important to the man I was living with than any image in a poem. How amazing that, at the age of forty-four, this was my first real experience of what it meant to be cherished. Above all, Leon gave me the one great gift that up until then had eluded me: the love and space and time to nurture myself and, in the process, to learn how to love not out of need but out of strength. With his encouragement, I wrote an autobiographical novel, *Nobody's Daughter*.

While we were still living in London, my mother died and I returned to Sydney for her funeral. Before leaving the cemetery, I walked over to my father's grave, which I had never visited. My heart lurched when I saw my name engraved on his stone: *Father of Aviva*. Whatever that curious notion of "closure" is, I certainly didn't feel it. Instead, I was overcome with a sense of outrage. How dare anyone entomb my name in granite? It was as if, against my will, I had been buried deep in that familiar and yet foreign Australian soil. I felt violated, bound to my parents and the country of my birth for all eternity.

I returned to London and, a few months later, moved back to Toronto with Leon and David. After David left home, we settled in Los Angeles. Each time I moved, I felt as if I had left some important part of myself behind and, like Lot's wife, kept looking backwards. Not an easy trait to live with, but I learned over the years that while some people go forward by going forward, I can only go forward by going back. When I was younger, I yearned to go to unfamiliar places, but the older I've become the more I yearn to return to my own personal Stations of the Cross: Sydney, Molyvos, Toronto, Montreal. For me, that need to revisit my past is really a chance to ask myself who I was then and who I am now.

That's why, when a close friend asked me to come back for Sydney Girls High School fiftieth reunion, I jumped at the chance. It was held at a downtown hotel and a gaggle of ladies in varying stages of decomposition greeted us as we walked through the lobby. We peered into one another's faces, trying to call up the young girls we once were. Apart from the obvious attrition of age, I realized that of the entire class of '49, there were few, minus some notable exceptions, who had made it outside the teaching profession. Sydney Girls High, the first state school in 1883 to offer girls the opportunity to study academic subjects, took only the best and the brightest, yet where were the doctors, the lawyers, the scientists, the professors, the writers, the artists? Could it have been that, like me, they had been unable to articulate lives for themselves that were outside the societal norm for that time? The cleverest girls—I was definitely not one of them—seemed to have led utterly predictable and safe lives, but it was amazing how much it stung to recognize Gloria McIntrye,* even though she was now a heavy-set matron with steel-gray hair. Not only did

*pseudonym

she actually own the name I had so passionately coveted, she had beat me out for the part of Lady Macbeth in our senior year, and I still found it hard to forgive her. It was also hard to assimilate the fact that everyone remembered me as a sunny, carefree girl, and I realized what a brilliant job of fakery I had pulled off.

That same need to revisit my past is why, although living in Los Angeles, I made so many trips back to Montreal to visit Irving, especially after he had been diagnosed with Alzheimer's. It was as if I wanted to hang onto those fragile filaments of memory of our life together that he still possessed, before they disappeared entirely. Despite our intensely difficult years, there remained between us a strong undercurrent of understanding and affection and a deep appreciation on my part of his poetry. It had taken many years to understand that we'd been meant to be friends, not lovers.

One of the most poignant visits I made was in response to a 4 a.m. phone call that came fifteen years after we'd separated. "You've been away on holiday too long!" insisted Irving. "It's time to come home and look after me." When I arrived, his Montreal home had so many objects left behind from my previous life with him that, again, I felt as if I'd been caught in a time warp. There was the Moroccan kilim we'd bargained for in a Marrakesh souk, the brass tray I'd haggled over in an Istanbul bazaar, the Balinese monkey mask, the small stone Buddha from Thailand. Even the kettle with the broken whistle, which I'd meant to have fixed all those years ago, still stood on top of the stove. Like my time in Sydney, I had a strong sense of time running backwards. Who was the person who'd lived that life for so many years and how much of her remained? Had she disappeared, or was she lurking around the perimeters?

It's taken a lifetime, but I finally believe that she has disappeared and that I no longer have to search for her. Traces still remain, though. I'm occasionally haunted by the thought that I never managed to fulfill myself as a writer and that even though my novel and a few children's stories were well received, I found writing much too painful and have retreated into the far more comfortable work of teaching and editing the writing of others.

There's a theory in quantum mechanics that posits the existence of parallel universes. Whenever we make a choice, so the theory goes, the multiple other choices we could have made exist in a parallel state. It's a theory that fascinates and intrigues me. Is there some plane of being in which I'm dancing *Swan Lake* in Covent Garden? Singing *Aida* in the Met? Playing the part of Lady Macbeth in the Old Globe? Being awarded the Pulitzer for having written the great American novel? And if it were possible to access those universes, would I choose to do so? It's tempting, but I don't think I would make that choice. The only parallel universe I would gladly access would be that in which I'm a responsible and sensitive mother to my son.

Increasingly, I find myself wondering where and when I'll die, although the truth is I suffer from a severe case of thanatophobia and don't want to die at any time. I remember reading somewhere—the words have squatted in my head like unwanted tenants—that if you don't want to die in the place where you're living, then you shouldn't be living there. If I *do* happen to die though, I want to be cremated instead of being nailed into a coffin, weighed down by earth and stone. As for my ashes, do I want them to be stored in Forest Lawn, that Disneyland of death? Scattered over the hardscrabble soil of

Sydney's Rookwood Cemetery? The snowy wastes of Toronto? The lonely little windswept cemetery of Molyvos? None of the above. Leon wants to be buried in our back garden, but I want to be thrown to the wind. Perhaps then some part of me will end up in all those places, as fragmented in death as I am in life.

Today, as I look into the mirror, I see all sorts of strange things like white hair and a body that gravity has compressed into odd folds. Who is this stranger staring back at me with the bags and sags, the pooches and pouches? Like so many of my friends, I've experienced the shock of catching a glimpse of myself in a mirror as I'm walking down a street, that disconcerting disconnect between self-image and objective reality. And I've certainly had my share of jarring moments, such as the time I casually glanced down into the mirrored surface of a coffee table and recoiled in horror when I saw the loosefleshed gargoyle staring back at me. In a flash, I understood why legions of women have insisted on the missionary position—it wasn't bourgeois inhibition, as I'd smugly assumed, but aesthetic necessity, a realistic appraisal of how scary you can look when you're on top. But however strange I may seem to myself, it will never rival the strangeness I felt as a child staring at myself in my mother's mirror.

I'm now able to accept the fact that I'll always feel fragmented, will always be full of regrets, always be haunted by the ghosts of past mistakes. I still wake up some nights in a cold sweat thinking of the hurts I've visited on my son who, because of his generous spirit and because he knows that despite everything, I've always loved him deeply, remains close to me. That closeness has given me the opportunity to apologize, an opportunity that is even more healing for me than for him. It's the least I can do. *Motion Sickness*, the memoir he has written about those years, describes his experiences, and, when people ask me if he was exaggerating, I answer—truthfully—

that, in fact, he's done the very opposite and has underplayed many of those dreaded "adventures."

Finally, at the age of seventy-five, I've come to the point where I can look into that mirror and nod to whatever selves I see reflected. They've become my familiars, pieces in a puzzle I'll never be able to complete.

The mirror that had always betrayed me no longer does.

AVIVA LAYTON is the author of the novel *Nobody's Daughter* and several children's books. Her essays have appeared in such anthologies as *The Other Woman*. She has taught literature at universities, colleges, and art schools and has reviewed plays, books, and film for newspapers, journals, and radio arts programs in the United States and Canada. Born in Sydney, Australia, the author lived for many years in Montreal, Toronto, and London. She currently resides in Los Angeles, where she works as a literary editor. Aviva is the mother of Canadian novelist David Layton and is married to author and architect Leon Whiteson.

ALL THE WRONG PLACES

Beverly Donofrio

The summer I was thirteen, the ugliest person I have ever seen walked into the cabin at our local swimming hole. Her long, thin nose seemed to stretch over her lips at the bottom edge of her face because her chin was missing. Her enormous eyes bugged out like a fly's. Her face was so horrible I had to memorize it. It's possible my mouth gaped open. The woman grabbed an armful of miniature Table Talk Pies, paid for them, then walked over to me on the sofa. "What are you looking at?" she snarled. "You think you're so pretty?

147

You'd better watch out, or you'll end up just like me." Then she turned and stomped out, letting the door slam behind her.

I was deeply shamed because I'd hurt the woman's feelings, but I was also frightened. Had she just cursed me? And what was I supposed to "watch out" for, anyway? Did she mean that if I wasn't a good person—if I lied, cursed, stole things, continued to hurt people's feelings; or if I were just not lucky, got a disease or into a near-fatal accident—I would end up like her?

That sighting so long ago began a vigil practiced often in my youth—and as I got older, perhaps every few years or so—of looking at my face in the mirror, wondering if it was morphing into that woman's. I do resemble her. I have the same olive coloring, a long nose, thin face, and, partly due to an overactive thyroid when I was in my teens, huge eyes. Plus, I was raised in an era of shame-shame Catholicism when we believed that God was just chomping at the bit to catch you in a sin so you could be tortured. I'd been rude, uncompassionate, and arrogant to stare at that woman, and not once in the immediate aftermath did I think to thank the Lord for the good fortune of my reasonably attractive face. Therefore, it was entirely possible that not only would God punish me, but had already punished the woman for something cruel she'd done.

When my first book came out, an arty photographer was hired by I think it was *Glamour* magazine to take my picture. The book was called *Riding in Cars with Boys*, and she snapped easily a hundred photos of me in various positions in a 1966 Chevy Impala. The photographer and I had chatted amiably, and I thought she liked me well enough—until I saw the photo. I'm leaning on my forearm staring out the car window, the bottom of my face cut off, my nose hanging down, my eyes like a fly's. I looked so much like that woman that I might have believed the curse had been accomplished, whimsically, and that it was finally over. But this never occurred to me at the time. And it has only occurred to me now, nearly twenty years later, to wonder: What did it mean that I'd come to look my ugliest, and publicly, the moment I believed all my dreams were finally coming true?

The dreams began as soon as we got a TV, when I was about four, and essentially amounted to this: a desire as painful as unrequited love, to be a star so famous people would wish they were me.

Neither of my parents graduated high school. My mother has never read a book in her life, including my own; and I recently learned that my father doesn't know what an index is. Children of Italian immigrants, they weren't even aware of half the things they were missing, but they were aware enough to feel inferior. Inferiority was a family affair. Perhaps by way of compensation, I convinced myself that I was born for great things.

When I was thirty-nine, *Riding in Cars with Boys*, the book I'd written about my life, was optioned by the movies before it had seen print. The Oscar-winning writer, director, and producer James L. Brooks flew me to the West Coast first class to meet him. A Mustang convertible awaited me at the airport, but it was my agent who drove me around Beverly Hills saying, "One day you'll live in a mansion. I've got a nose for talent. And you've got it. Believe me. You could own this town if you wanted." And I believed him, even though he also said, "I will always return your calls."

Perhaps ex-teenaged mothers are more gullible than most. Getting pregnant in high school did not encourage high self-esteem. But since I was stuck home with a kid at eighteen, the library became my university, and books saved my life. Soon, I decided to be a writer instead of an actor, because writing didn't require babysitters. Then the sixties hit town, late, in 1968, and the top of my head blew off. By 1971, I was able to add wild, promiscuous hippie; hitchhiker; shoplifter; divorcée;

welfare mom; and convicted felon to the ways I saw myself. And then fatso. After my name was splashed on the front page of the newspaper for being part of a drug ring—not true—I gained thirty pounds: rather than one piece of toast dripping with butter and slathered with raspberry jam, I ate four. Fat and ashamed of myself, I avoided the mirror and slept every chance I got.

Eighteen years later, driving by the Beverly Hillbillies' mansion with my agent, I pictured myself walking the red carpet on the movie's opening night—and at the big bash afterward, meeting Judith Rossner, the author of *Waiting for Mr. Goodbar* and other best sellers of the '70s and '80s. I would take a sip of my drink, look her up and down with icy bug-out eyes and say, "Judith *who*?" She was the famous writer who'd failed me from the MFA creative writing program at Columbia University. I had never met her but had chosen her to read my thesis—an admittedly rough draft of *Riding*—because I considered her a popular novelist and not literary. Which was the best I believed I could ever ask of my own writing.

If I hadn't been bawling hysterically when I read her critique, I might have laughed at the irony when I read, "This is not literary." She accused me of creating "cardboard, cut-out characters from a situation comedy going from one implausible situation to the next." I'd written truly about my life and called it fiction, and she thought I'd made it all up. She was wrong about that, but she was right when she said, "It's easy to see why Beverly Donofrio's energy has been mistaken for talent." I was an imposter, a poseur, a dreamer with dreams way bigger than my gifts.

Fallen from the impossible heights of my own grandiosity,

I gave up writing and took a full-time job for only the second time in my life—as copy editor on a magazine. And for the first time in my life, I got real. I had vowed that as a writer I'd work only part-time jobs to leave myself time enough to write, and that I would only write literature: novels, short stories, or poetry. While I was pursuing my lofty dreams, my thirteen-year-old son and I lived on pizza and Chinese, worried every month about making the rent, tolerated toothaches until I could save enough for the dentist. I'd been forcing my son to suffer deprivations so I could pursue my dreams, which had less to do with creating great literature than with being perceived as great by others.

I worked two jobs: proofreading on Sundays at Time Inc. and copyediting at the magazine during the week. After a few months of closely reading the submissions, I was pretty sure that I could write as well as at least some of the magazine's writers. Soon I was contributing short pieces. And then I published an essay in the *Village Voice*, which won me a contract to write my first book.

After my agent dropped me back at the Beverly Hilton, I looked at myself in the mirror. I was wearing a designer outfit I'd bought in Soho with part of the $100,000 I'd been advanced from the $450,000 I would eventually be paid. The advance was probably more money than I'd earned in my entire life, and I was nearly forty. My eyes were big, intense, and a little scared looking. I tried to make them soft and deserving, the eyes of a woman entitled to admiration and love.

I think it must have been only a few years after the chinless woman, when I was fifteen, that I sat in front of the mirror and imagined an angel sitting on one shoulder and the devil on the other. I decided that, if I had the choice, I'd be the devil, no question, because suffering was much more interesting than kindness. There'd been a show on TV called *The Naked City* that started with a voiceover, "There are ten million stories in the Naked City." I'd thought how in any given second a baby was being born dead, someone had just been stabbed, shot, run over, stood up at the altar, how a kid was being beaten by bullies and another just fell out a window.

I even moved to the Naked City after I graduated college at twenty-eight, and then stayed for thirteen years, on 12th Street and Avenue A. It was known as Alphabet City but could easily have been called Crack Depot, Junkie Haven, Hello Hell. My landlady's boyfriend was stabbed under my window and under my own eyes. Men fought using garbage can lids as shields. A sea of boys rumbled in front of the middle school across the road, which was next to a church I never entered. Once, on my way home, I passed a shooting victim, a tarp-covered corpse on my corner, roped off by the police. The guy's brand-new white Puma sticking out. At home I wept, thinking of the guy's mother and how she probably didn't even know her son was dead. Jeanette, the Frenchwoman who lived in the building next door, devolved from a lovely middle-aged woman with curled red hair, walking her little dog, to a ragged, makeup-smeared, hair-matted wreck, mumbling to herself, and without her dog.

It wasn't long after the agent drove me around Hollywood that I was feeling almost as wrecked as Jeanette. I'd expected that success would make people love me, but it hadn't happened. In fact, my boyfriend had just dumped me. Jim Brooks, a Hollywood gorilla, had thought me talented enough to advance me money to write another book—and to give me a contract to write the screenplay of the book I hadn't yet written. I was supposed to be ecstatically happy, but I was as lonesome as homelessness.

I'd read books on Buddhism and knew about craving and how insatiable desire is, how even if you get what you think you want, it will never make you happy because you'll only want more, and then more, and bigger, and better. I theorized that the only thing that could fill the hole of longing howling in me was love, and oh, so slowly, I came to interpret love as God. And THIS God I wanted to believe in.

Because it looked like the movie was finally getting made and I was a producer, I moved out to Los Angeles and was given an office on the Sony Pictures lot. This move coincided with the beginning of my spiritual journey.

At a party, I met a woman screenwriter who had won an Academy Award. I was writing my second memoir and working on it daily. I asked the screenwriter if she wrote every day, too. And she said, "Honey, if I wrote every day, I'd own this town." And something snapped. "Who would want to?" popped into my head.

I consulted on many of the twenty-five drafts of the script and then, when the movie was green-lighted, I went to dinner with Drew Barrymore, who was to play me. We met in New York City at the Cowgirl Hall of Fame, where the margarita-besotted crowd parted like the Red Sea.

Drew was the star I had wanted to be.

The crowd calling out, "We love you, Drew," felt like love. But it wasn't love, it was adulation. How confusing would that be? I'm not proud to say, I felt proud to be seen with her. I caught myself, and soon after, I bowed out, left town and even the country. I didn't trust myself. No telling how long before I'd start lusting after the wrong thing again.

It is now seven years after the movie that did not make me famous was released. For the past year I have lived as a lay member—a hermit of sorts—of a Carmelite community high up in the mountains of Colorado. I try to keep love present in every moment and action of my days, which includes washing the dishes and scrubbing the toilet. I am never successful, but I do usually remember once or twice or ten times in a day to try. I pray, which for me means being still and listening in the silence. And sometimes in my prayer I feel, more than actually remember, a very early time, a time before I came to believe I was not good enough. Perhaps the time lasted only until the age of two. Back then, the sun, the clouds, the moon, the stars were all inside of me, so were birdsong and the tree so majestically tall in my yard. I loved them all and they loved me, but it wasn't like that. They *were* me and I was them.

This rare feeling, when it comes, is fleeting, but it makes me think that the sky is not a ceiling. There are no heights to reach and no rock bottom on which to fall.

I hadn't remembered the chinless woman for a few years, until I began thinking about writing this essay. Now, as I look at my own face in the mirror, the one that used to belong to the girl my mother called a pip and a pill. Who used to line her eyes like Cleopatra, wear fishnet stockings under skirts that barely covered her wazoo. The one who could dance until the sun came up and give a look so contemptuous it would wilt you. The one who Drew Barrymore does not look like. The selfish mother who would lay down her life for her son. The grandmother who looks like an old shoe because she's ready to drop from chasing around her three-year-old pip of a grandson. The hermit on the mountain who sometimes can feel on her face the same expression she had when she was two—of wonder and joy at the whisper in a breeze. We're all here in the mirror—the woman with no chin on her face, too.

BEVERLY DONOFRIO's first memoir, *Riding in Cars with Boys*, has been translated into fifteen languages and transformed into a popular motion picture. Her second memoir, *Looking for Mary* (or, *The Blessed Mother and Me*), began as a documentary on NPR and was chosen as a Discover Book at Barnes & Noble. Her first children's books, *Mary and the Mouse, the Mouse and Mary*, and *Thank You, Lucky Stars*, appeared in 2007, and a sequel to the *Mouse* book is due out soon. She is an award-winning radio commentator and can be heard on such programs as *All Things Considered*. Her personal essays have appeared in many anthologies, as well as in national newspapers and magazines. Donofrio is currently a lay Carmelite hermit at Nada Hermitage in Colorado, where she is happily at work on her third memoir, whose working title is *Meanwhile, Back at the Monastery*. Her Web site is http://www.beverlydonofrio.com.

LAURIE STONE

MY TICKET TO RIDE

Richard Toon

BIRMINGHAM, ENGLAND, 1971

I t's a ten-minute walk to the bus stop and a forty-minute ride to the city center atop the double-decker bus. Other people read the paper or smoke. I clear a hole in the misted window and look out. Below, tobacconists and green-grocers are opening for the day along the Coventry Road. Armies of office workers, like me, are waiting in the drizzle for buses. Quietly, under my breath, I sing the Beatles tune "A Day in the Life," the bit where Paul

157

McCartney warbles about the workaday routine, and I retrace the steps I've just taken: getting up, finding my coat and hat, rushing to the bus and just making it. And someone does speak, and I go into my own dream, and in it I never get Marylyn* pregnant when we are seventeen. I don't marry her. Trevor* isn't born. It hasn't all fallen apart three years later. I don't move away from Syston and get a job.

I'm not on this bus going to work—and nowhere. The song is about a lucky man who makes the grade, but how does he do it? The lyrics aren't specific, and the image films over like the hole I've made in the window. It's the dream of an altered state, like the ones I induce with marijuana on weekends—an escape without aspiration.

I'm living in Small Heath, Birmingham, a grim district furrowed by streets of nineteenth-century blackened terraced homes. I rent a second-floor flat from the Mulvaneys, an aging Irish couple who have stepped out of a Dickens novel—my world feels like a Dickens novel. I was born in the English Midlands, in the middle of the century, and yet, as I look back, so much that I experienced unfolds in Victorian settings, as if England existed in some strange time-warp after the war, which I now understand it did.

I have two chilly rooms at the top of the stairs. One is a combined kitchen/bathroom, the other a bed-sitter with a metered gas fire that needs a stack of shillings I'm too poor to feed. Even if I could, a shilling buys only twenty minutes of heat, and heat isn't exactly what radiates out, more like a gasp of warm breath too weak to raise the pulse on the permanently dank, damp surroundings. Mrs. Mulvaney's deeply lined, sallow face and her mouth slashed with red lipstick announce she's had a hard time of it. As she speaks, a cigarette stub

*pseudonym

quivers in her lips, sporting a precarious inch of ash. I find its trail through my place when I return home from work, for as soon as I leave she lets herself in and pokes around my scant belongings: a stack of paperbacks, a pile of laundry by the unmade bed, a transistor radio. When confronted with the evidence, she swears she's innocent. "Saints preserve us," she cries, looking at the ceiling in their direction. "I've not so much as got a key." Adding to my sense of confinement, the hood of the gas fire is stamped with a small swastika. When I point this out to the Mulvaneys, hoping for confirmation that life is as inexplicable and perverse as I am finding it, they peer down nearsightedly and say they can't see it.

I am watching the Mulvaneys as intently as they are scrutinizing me, for, pathetic as it is to admit, they supply what passes for human contact. Mr. Mulvaney, many years retired from his job, performs a pantomime of going to work. Each weekday morning at seven I hear him say "Cheerio, Mother," through the thin walls. Do they have children somewhere? None visits. I eat my breakfast of cold milk and shredded wheat, perched over the bathtub-cum-dining-table that looks out onto the backyard garages. In need of repair, they have taken to leaning together like drunken friends coming home from the pub. A few haughty pigeons peck at the edge of an oily puddle as Mr. Mulvaney, briefcase in hand, finds his old Rover, backs it out, steps outside again to kick the tires, climbs back in, drinks steaming tea from the yellow plastic cup he unscrews from his thermos flask, and settles in to read the *Daily Telegraph*. I never see the car driven in the street.

Daily, too, Mrs. Mulvaney, armed with a feather duster, cleans the false ceilings she's gone to the uncharacteristic expense of installing in her ground floor of the house. Every Saturday I descend to pay the rent with crisp pound notes doled out directly from the slim brown envelope of my wage packet, my name written on the outside in blue-black ink. My hair brushes the ceiling (fortunately, clean) as I lay pictures of the queen across her upturned palm, and I feel anonymous—the boarder, the lodger, a minor character who gets killed off or falls in love and emigrates to Australia, a nameless somebody plugged into other people's stories. I feel excited by the awfulness. It's almost a reverse glamour, for I am free and no one knows me, but I am also skimming along, and I fear I could disappear in a way that freezes me if I dwell on it. Or I could become the Mulvaneys. What really separates us? Is this the life Marylyn and I, had we stayed together, would have cobbled together through inertia and lost opportunities? Who am I to want more? Who am I, full stop?

And why is this memory coming back? Maybe it's because I was alone then, as I have seldom been, as I am alone again, and in this state I like to taste my narrow escapes—the times I was dangling over a precipice, or just running.

The night before I leave Marylyn, she goes off to a club to dance and drink. As gray, watery light drains the darkness, I'm awakened by a car engine throbbing outside the house. Through the bedroom curtains, I see her step out of a green sports car, pulling on the shoulder-strap of the paisley mini-dress she loves to dance in. I see her wave and smile to the driver, a stranger, as the car moves away. I go back to bed, feeling a pang of jealousy, but it's not deep, for I have never loved her. I hear water running in the sink downstairs, and then she slips in beside me. I pretend to be asleep and soon hear her breathing deeply. As I rise and dress, Marylyn's eyes are still closed, and Trevor is in his little bed in the back room. Everything is peaceful. I work a normal day and never return.

How have we arrived here? I may not know the why, but I can replay the events. The camera goes "Whap!" The bulb flashes, and suddenly I'm beyond sound and vision—no wedding photographer, no friends smiling and congratulating me with a slap on the back, no mother and father looking strained and tired, no bride appearing radiant in her floor-length, powder-blue wedding dress—just a silence, and in the center of it an overwhelming realization that I have made a terrible mistake. "Whap!" the camera goes again, and I am back, offering a soft smile of surrender. The moment of clarity—half a second at most—will be forgotten for many years.

It's a June day in 1968. Marylyn is five months pregnant, though her dress conceals it handily. She stands five-foot-two, and her dark auburn hair is cut in a pageboy that frames a round, open face. Despite her sugary diet, she has Chiclets-white teeth she considers as dazzling as a model's. She paints her full, kissable mouth with Mary Quant pink lipstick, and she has bright clear eyes done up with liner and mascara, and notable in that one is blue and the other brown—in fact, she's known in the village as "the girl with the different-colored eyes." I like that her breasts are small, and even more that she is happy for me to feel them as soon as I try.

And so, like dominoes falling over, we move from snogging on buses to screwing against the door of the council house where she lives with her mother and six sisters, to me saying, "I think I love you," unconsciously stealing the lyric from the Jim Morrison song, although Marylyn has not asked for my love, does not require it. And I agree to marry her when she tells me she is pregnant, even though I'm not certain that the baby is mine. I don't really care, because what I want is to be with her body, to have sex with her in a bed whenever possible. And I am looking for a place to put myself, and the model of my parents, tucked away together in their house where they raise their kids, looks cozy and not suffocating. I haven't done well at school. I have a hunch I'm smart, but I resist learning by rote and I've had little encouragement to express my kind of mind. I want to be held, and that yearning for safety—if that's the right word for it—will prove perilous.

After leaving Marylyn, I stay with various friends, each for several days, moving from flat to flat with the few belongings I have taken from the house, little more than a change of clothes, really. I have no plans, just wait for the next thing to happen after what I've set in motion. This is what I will do at other pivotal times: launch myself into space and feel like I'm riding an escalator up and down, with no desire to step off. After a couple of weeks, I run out of people willing to let me sleep on their sofas and wash my shirt in their sinks. I'm alone with a couple of carrier bags to drag around as company. I walk south for no reason I recall, out of the center of the city, and after a few miles I'm relieved to arrive at Victoria Park, where I sit, panicked and elated. I have five pounds in my pocket, and it doesn't occur to me that I am desperately without means. I wish Trevor were there to hold, but I'm glad Marylyn isn't.

As it gets dark, a fine rain begins to fall, and I head for the pavilion across the cricket grounds. I find a telephone box there that smells, as they all do, of stale cigarette smoke. Beneath the low-watt bulb, I push four pennies into the slot for a call, and I hear my dad answer the phone, "Hello, 6637054," exactly as he has a thousand times. It's a wonderfully comforting sound, and I'm thinking everything's fine now. I press button A, and the coins clatter down into the black box. I say, "Hello, Dad. I left Marylyn," and he says, "I know, your mother's been down. Marylyn told her." And I ask softly, "Can I stay with you for a day or so, while I get things sorted out?" And there's a silence on the line for a moment or two, and I hear my heart beating and wonder if he can hear it, too, and he says, "No, son, I don't think that's a good idea. You know what you have to do." It's not said bitterly, rather as an obvious fact, almost tenderly. And I know he means: Go back to your wife and child, even though you are a child, too. I cannot—and will not—save you from your own bad choices. I don't argue with him, just say, "Okay, Dad, I'll call in a few days." And I know I will not return to Marylyn. It has all been played out, and whatever comes next lies ahead.

As I put down the phone, I feel like one of those villains in old movies who, once he's been shot, looks down at the wound in disbelief and turns his hand over to see the blood on his fingertips and only then realizes: This time it's for keeps. And I say to myself, right there, out loud in the telephone box, as if I'm on stage and there's an audience, I say, "Looks like you're on your own." And I spend the night moving around the park, looking for a place to keep warm, and as the light starts to come I find a building on the far side where I huddle down in the doorway and sleep for a couple of hours.

In Birmingham, near where I work for the water department—issuing hose-pipe licenses, don't ask—the city's art museum beckons. It's like the other municipal museums my parents took me to as a child: deserted and by and large pretty dingy, though free and warm. I like its quiet and separateness from bustling New Street, and I take to visiting daily, moving swiftly through the gallery spaces without keeping track of where I am until finding a place to sit. Then, if no attendant is on duty, I pull chunks off my sandwich and contemplate whatever is on view. One day, I find myself in front of John Millais's painting *The Blind Girl*, which, according to the provenance nailed to the frame, is over a hundred years old, but to me the paint still appears wet. During the year I live in Birmingham, I return many times to contemplate its vibrant details: the butterfly on the blind girl's shawl, the crows eating in the field, the village on the horizon, the accordion on the blind girl's lap, the clenched grip of the two girls in the foreground as the younger, sighted child looks back across the open field toward the storm. On this first encounter, I concentrate on the two rainbows that the blind girl can't see and the other girl doesn't see, given the way her shawl is draped. But *I* can see them. I see two arcs of color, one for each soul, containing the promise of a better world to come, and I think, *Me, too,* in a quite material way, for I am not religiously musical. There is nothing subtle in the message; it fairly hits me between the eyes. I chew on the sandwich I have smuggled in and start to laugh. I have already met Meg, whom I will marry next, and she is at university, and I will begin to study and eventually gain acceptance at a university, too, and the government will pay for my education. I will study philosophy and eventually earn a PhD in museum studies, for museums will remain transformative spaces throughout my life. I laugh rather too loudly, and the sound echoes in the halls, and soon an attendant, awakening like a sleeping giant, walks in and, seeing me eating and laughing at a blind girl, orders me to leave.

Thirty years later, in my house in Phoenix where my wife, Suzanne,* and I live, my Mum and Dad will come for a rare visit, and we will talk about old times in England. Dad is that England. It's ninety-nine degrees out, but inside he will wear a Marks & Spenser brown wool cardigan, because he finds the air-conditioning chilly. He will seem frail as he pulls his body toward me on the sofa.

We will talk about the time I left Maryln and moved to

---

*pseudonym

Birmingham, and he will say, "I'm sorry for not saying you could come home. It was a mistake I have always regretted." He will put his hand on my knee for a second and then throw his arms up a little, adding, "Yes, it's a long time ago, but there you are." And I will think about the apologies I have yet to make.

PHOENIX, ARIZONA, 2008

So you find yourself falling in love and you can't just kiss it good-bye. You can't walk away and pretend it never happened. You've been split open, and you find yourself going to extreme lengths to stay in touch. You come back from the artist colony and discover your clothes no longer fit, the pictures on the wall belong to someone else, the body next to you is a stranger, and even odder, the person next to your wife is a stranger, too. It takes you a while, but you tell Suzanne the truth, and then you leave your life and home. *Again.* Your friends and family say you're repeating a pattern. You recognize this. Pattern recognition is what you're known for in your intellectual work. You left Marylyn, then Meg, and now Suzanne, but each relationship was different. You and Suzanne were together for more than twenty years, and you were close and warm and dependent on each other, but it was time for both of you to feel more alive while aliveness was still an option. You don't care about looking like the cliché of a man in a midlife crisis, because as far as you are concerned every stage of life is a crisis. You have been an insulin-dependent diabetic since your early days with Meg, and at the time you didn't expect to make it into your fifties with all your extremities intact. But you have, weirdly; against the odds, you have.

So in time Laurie comes to live with you in Arizona, and at

first you are both on your best behavior and take turns going nuts. It's your turn the day she drives to pick you up from work and gets a flat. She pulls up slowly, and you see the car has a wobble. You decide your insurance is out of date, even though you remember putting the card in the glove compartment. You call for roadside assistance and are assured it's on its way. Rain begins. You sigh. Laurie is nice to you. You know it can't last. You keep checking the rearview mirror for the repair truck, certain he won't find you. You will run out of quarters for the meter and have to abandon the car. You will get a ticket, be arrested, and deported back to England. You are weighing the option of fleeing the United States right now, but you have no way to get to the airport.

Laurie is nothing like Suzanne, and you think you want this: the excitement, the intimacy. But once the boundaries are broken that you have waited your whole life to see dissolved, watch out. You express concern about your nose hairs, for example. You have a distinctive nose that turns up slightly at the tip, so it's easy to see into your nostrils, and Laurie remarks that the hairs inside are sprouting into little tufts, like an old toothbrush. When she approaches you with scissors, you head for the Target in search of a battery-operated trimmer, and you can't find where they're stocked, so Laurie asks directions from a bewildered pharmacist counting pills. "Where are those things that trim nose hairs?" she asks in a voice loud enough for everyone in the megastore to hear, or so it seems, and turning, she bellows, "Does it have a name?" By then you are down another aisle, pretending not to know her.

You alternate between being together and separating for periods while Laurie goes to artist residencies, like the one where you met in Saratoga Springs. You were working on a book of essays about museum spaces, and you started writing in notebooks together. You are enjoying the challenge of this creativity and the way it is opening you up, but Laurie is not easy and you fight. She has opinions about everything, and you are afraid she will blame you for luring her to a cultural desert, even though she enjoys the actual desert with rocks and cacti. You fear that after the pain you've caused to be with her, she will retreat to New York, where you don't want to live because of the cold, the cost, and the muggers who threatened you when you lived there with Suzanne. You feel this relationship holds a gun to your head, forcing you to live up to the promises you've made to yourself over a lifetime. It's now or never, and the pressure is making your head spin.

I am looking for a stone tablet, the size and shape of an open book, installed in a glass box somewhere in the Phoenix Art Museum. I saw it a year ago with Laurie. At first the movement on the surface of the small, archaeological slab looked like flowing cuneiform script, but as I leaned in I saw that the "letters" were actually a shadowy projection of tiny human figures. The piece was astonishing, both concrete and metaphoric, and I saw myself on the stone, walking through England and across the ocean to the States.

I have come here to sympathize with objects lifted out of their natural biographies and presented for contemplation. I have come here to turn that gaze on myself. It's a Sunday morning, and a few watchful attendants saunter through the galleries, ignoring the art. I'm just beyond the lobby, the only visitor, and I'm already lost. I turn the map around and around. In museums, I can't locate "here," and, of course, I'm too shy to ask for "the stone thing."

Last time, with Laurie, we swished along together, hands touching, clothes brushing. I could have asked for anything, the way I asked for love and desire and received them. She described a story she was writing about a man who emerges from the white cloud of the collapsed World Trade Towers and keeps on going; he slips the knot, walking away from the life he's known. "I have the character and setting," she said, "but not the plot." I thought she must be thinking of me, leaving someone I cared for after twenty-two years of marriage, but Laurie insists she had the idea before we met.

I've been on my own for a week. Laurie is away writing, and when we talked on the phone this morning she said there are only three weeks left to go. I need to learn to be alone. Laurie, who was used to sleeping by herself, has accommodated to my sleep patterns. I need to fit into her waking patterns: her need for solitude and not to be disturbed by me.

In museums—mirrors of what we were, what we value, and what we want to be—I think about the artifacts and actions that mirror my life. Laurie suggests it's time to write my apology to Trevor. I agree, and pain sweeps through me. I remember the last time we spoke. It must be ten years ago. Out of the blue the phone rings, and a voice says, "'Ey up, it's Trevor." A man's voice with a working-class British accent I don't recognize, and he launches in and tells me about the garage he works in and his nights down at the pub, and I'm back in Birmingham, smelling the cabbage soup that would seep into the hall as I passed the Mulvaneys' door. I'm back in the life I scrambled out of, wishing I could have taken my boy along, too. Is this my boy? Trevor doesn't specify why he's calling, although he mentions he has a daughter who wants to speak to me. I don't catch her name. He says, "What the fuck, I thought, I'd give yer a ring and see what yer thought." He apologizes for not "speaking proper," and I feel his awkwardness is more honest than mine. I listen, but I don't have it in me to apologize to him for all those years of neglect. I sent a few birthday cards, and then nothing for a long, long time. I don't tell him that when I first left Marylyn, I tried to take him with me, but no one would rent a room to a boy holding the hand of a smaller boy. His voice reminds me of my shame and regret, and the pity I feel for myself chokes off all other emotion. Kill the messenger.

Why did Trevor and I quarrel and end the call badly? He was almost thirty. Shortly after Marylyn and I divorced, she married a man I didn't like to think of as Trevor's father although, in fact, he raised him. The quarrel involved a story Marylyn invented about our parting, and Trevor recited it, a romantic tale of having married too young and being in love but unable to accept the responsibilities. I balked at this version because it served Marylyn, and that, as my Mum would say, "led to words." I had an impulse to tell Trevor the truth: that maybe I wasn't his father. I wanted to be rid of comforting stories, but I thought it would hurt him to say this. A few weeks before, I was on the phone with my Mum when out of the blue she asked if it had ever occurred to me that Trevor might not be my son. "He doesn't look like anyone in the family." It was one of those safety nets people in my family whisper to you, in which you are invited to see yourself as a victim. To accept the dodge diminishes you, though, because it's a lie—a lie that in this case might, factually, be the truth. "What difference does paternity make?" I came back, arguing that I'd assumed the responsibility and hadn't followed through, regardless of what a DNA test might confirm. I felt frustrated keeping quiet to Trevor, but I didn't feel I had a right to push my understanding on him, and as I look back, I think he interpreted my discomfort as lack of interest in him.

Laurie believes that words can never come too late and that children who are left always think it's their fault. The apology I owe might sound like this: "Trevor, I am deeply sorry I had to leave you, but I did not love your mother as you did and, I hope, still do. I saw an opportunity out of a hopeless situation, and I took it, leaving you behind. It had nothing to do with loving you. You were all the pleasure in my life at the time. I can't see you as the man you are now. He is a stranger to me. I see you only as that three-year-old child on the little tricycle in the garden forty years ago. You have a bewildered look on your upturned face as I lean down to say good-bye. 'Why are you crying, Daddy?' you ask, with a softness I see no trace of, in the man you have become. I feel ashamed because I left you to a stepfather I didn't like and it seems that the part of me that was part of you has worn away. I don't tell you why I'm crying, just kiss you and turn to leave."

The man on the phone tells me I have two grandchildren, and inside I say, "I don't." Inside I say, "I have no child; there are no children of children." I think of all the moves I've made, all the dreams snatched, all the opportunities jumped for, all the escape hatches slipped into. I get educated, move through three marriages, out of poverty, out of my country, and on to new life. A strong impulse to keep moving develops, lest the past catches up and demands its due, and I fear I still have nothing to offer: no apology to make or justification to give.

I find the stone in the glass box and copy the label's text into my notebook. "Michal Rovner, steel vitrine with glass, stone, and DVD video projection. Born in Israel, 1957. Lives in New York." The light is on, and the figures are moving across the stone. I take my place among the wanderers, and we are walking on city streets and in the Negev Desert. I am walking in the Sonoran Desert in Arizona, and we are looking at the places where we started and those we roamed to. I am searching for a way to feel embraced and yet free, and it makes me laugh, the impossible pull of that, welcome to the human race. I am looking for the museum of myself, where I can eat a sandwich and stare ahead, and it comes to me, a memory from a time when I had what I am trying to get back to: when I was alone, yet still belonged somewhere; when I was expressive and yearned for an unknown world.

It's 1955, and I am five, and inside me is a jazz record, a spinning disc, the sound loose as a bead of mercury in a warm palm, slippy and jumping. We live in Bury, Lancashire, in the north of England. The war is ten years over, but there's still rationing of coal, and the objects that fill homes are more reminiscent of the 1920s and '30s than the new designs of the '50s. Just about every terraced house in Bury has a small front parlor where, in pride of place, stands a gramophone. Times are tight, so most of the players are wind-up cabinets; only the posh can afford electric pickups. Uncle Freddie instructs me on how to crank the arm, place the heavy shellac disc on the green baize turntable, adjust the speed to "fast"—roughly 78 rpm— and gently lower the heavy-headed needle onto the record that is spinning crazily. It clunks into the groove, and then by a miracle of physics I don't understand, music pours brightly into the stiff and dark room. I'm beside myself with pleasure. It's my first altered brain state, and I feel made of jazz, a mercury blob of rhythms. I play each short song over and over. At the end, the needle skates around in the center of the disc, clicking impatiently to begin again.

The music available is of two types: Uncle Freddie's novelty songs and my dad's collection of American big-band jazz, picked up during the war he spent in Europe, including serving with Patton's troops. The novelty tunes are sung by George Formby and Gracie Fields. George plays ukulele and sings comic ditties with a northern nasal twang, the songs punctuated with his catchphrase, "Turned out nice again." Gracie sings "I'm a Lassie from Lancashire," layering in high-soprano trills. But it's the jazz and swing that send me to the secret place inside myself I think of as America: Ellington's "Take the 'A' Train," Basie's "One O'clock Jump," Arty Shaw's "Deep Purple," Glenn Miller's "Don't Sit under the Apple Tree." I memorize the words without knowing their meaning. On the

B-side of "Take the 'A' Train" is "At a Dixie Roadside Diner." I have no idea where Dixie is, what a diner is, or why it's on the roadside, but I love this place in America, because it swings with cool and sophistication that call me.

In order to liberate the house from my playing and to dispose of the gramophone cabinet, which has developed a case of wood worm, Freddie places the guts of the contraption in a cardboard box and sets me up in the alley at the back of his house. I stack the records in their deco-designed paper sleeves against the outhouse and proceed to play jazz to anyone who happens by, plus a few dogs that are sniffing about. Adults on the way to the pub smile and shake their heads, while the kids look on embarrassed for the child playing weird music for no discernable reason. After a while, even the dogs shuffle off looking bored. And there I am in the back streets of Bury, playing Duke Ellington to an indifferent world, and I feel just fine about it, the solitude and pleasure. I drag the box from one end of Hulme Street to the other until the bottom frays away and Freddie comes by and says in that broad Lancashire dialect that will die with him, "Thy needs 'tuther box, our Bud." And he brings me one, and I play the songs, day after day, as long as the boxes last.

RICHARD TOON was born in England. Since 2004, he has worked as a senior research analyst at the Morrison Institute for Public Policy, at Arizona State University, where he also teaches museum studies. His essays have appeared in such publications as *Museum Revolutions*, *Reshaping Museum Space*, and *Curator*. In 2006, he was awarded a residency at the artist colony Yaddo in Saratoga Springs, New York, where he worked on *Pictures at an Exhibition*, an essay collection, including stories of an English boyhood and meditations on jumping across classes and cultures. He is currently at work on *Sugar Time*, a memoir about diabetes and the British class system, and *Unmarked Trail: A Romance in Stories and a Guide to Setting Up a Writing Partnership*, in collaboration with Laurie Stone.

IRA BLOCK

TRUE MIRROR

Nancy Weber

I'll never win second place in a beauty contest, but I look better for sixty-six than I did for sixteen, twenty-six, fifty-six. Asymmetrical eyes and mouth needed decades to make friends with my nose, so prominent that a plastic surgeon I met just after college offered to reinvent it gratis. "My nose for news," protested this girl reporter, freshly installed on the amusement desk of the *New York Post*. Streisand wowed Broadway about the same time, and I loved her for saying she would never have a nose job because it might affect

175

her voice. I couldn't—can't—carry a tune in a bucket. Imagine my glee when a fan screeched "Barbra!" as I swanned down the steps from Kenneth Battelle's fabled salon, where my ever-indulgent parents treated me to the haircut Kenneth had designed for her: a chin-length bob ironed straight, shiny and swinging, positively Protestant. I graciously waggled two fingers at the fan, then darted through traffic across Fifty-fourth before I was asked to sing or sign. Couldn't wait to tell the story to a certain Marty, a trust-fund hippie, who seemed to think he was doing me a favor by taking me out. "Streisand is beautiful," he said coldly. "You, at your best, are cute."

Grew into my nose, grew out of jerks, and, lucky me, the dermatologists who'd treated me for runny red teenage acne were telling the truth about the future. "Oily skin is an old woman's best friend. Someday you'll be grateful. No wrinkles." Does "someday" register on the teen brain, its whorls conscripted, every one, into dealing with the impossibly complicated present? No. I thought I would ooze forever. My father used to lubricate the pieces of his trout rod by rubbing them alongside my nose, that nose. My father, the kindest of men.

Not beautiful, not pretty, and, really, I was never cute, then or now. So it's gratifying when an old friend or first husband accuses me of looking terrific and asks, "Did you do something to your face?"

Well, no. More a matter of my face doing something to me.

At age sixty-one, I saw myself for the first time. Blame it on the sushi at Jewel Baka, a sleek bamboo tunnel of a restaurant with maybe a dozen tables on East Fifth Street. In the last months of my second marriage, the son of that union, then seventeen, took consolation from the otoro; for me, it was the mackerel and much-unfiltered sake. By wonderful chance, a gallery across the street caught our attention one evening. In the window was a display of mirrors set inside brightly colored cubes. We peered at ourselves and went, "Wow." What—whom—were we seeing? It wasn't exactly a funhouse effect, but it wasn't reflection as we knew it. Something was so shockingly different that both of us were dizzied. And oddly elated.

The gallery was closed, but a poster explained all. We were looking at ourselves in a True Mirror: actually two mirrors placed at a ninety-degree angle to each other and fastened so meticulously that the seam disappeared from view. Instead of reversing our images, as normal mirrors do, the True Mirror let us see ourselves as others saw us, for the first time in our lives.

We returned the next day and bought a tabletop edition, a twelve-inch cube, painted teal, that appeared to have a mirror set deep inside it. And we learned more. Technology for the nonreversing mirror was patented in the late nineteenth century, but it took a modern nuclear physicist, John Walter, working with "space-age" glue, to turn theory into beautiful objects. True Mirror is the result of his collaboration with Catherine Walter, his sister and a cultural anthropologist, who has contributed theory and run the gallery. (It subsequently closed for good, but the factory abides.) The Walters have written extensively about politicians and the significance of their left or right hair parts; they call Barack Obama a *charismatic non-parter*. True Mirror has been exhibited and discussed at psychoanalytic seminars and the Whitney Biennial; it hangs in the restrooms of funky downtown New York bars.

Some people cannot stand their images in the True Mirror. Others—I'm one of them—all but have a Narcissus moment. It's not about noses or skin or the angling, the glue. For me—and I suspect for many—joy derives from the giddy power of self-definition. This is a precious freedom: no longer needing to be told how you look and therefore who you are.

Blame my mother, but of course, that I grew up conflating the seeming and the being, the haircut and the soul.

I've kept few physical mementos from my childhood, and they're stored in a jumble, but I can always put my hands on the faded pink satin album titled *Precious Moments* that must have been a newborn gift to my parents. Much too sentimental for their taste, they filled in few of the pages. Tellingly, there's a pasted-on receipt for a five-dollar donation to Russian War Relief, along with my official birth announcement and some sepia nursery snapshots. (I was young, but they were *really* young.) And then there's a bit of Shakespeare in the space labeled *Mother's Message*. "This above all, to thine own self be true," she wrote in her fine hand—the tall, thin, blond, cigarette-smoking ex-Commie painter champion golfer, Caroline.

There was a space for *Father's Message*, but my darling daddy, Saul, left it blank. I was born in 1942, six years before Carl Sandburg published his novel, *Remembrance Rock*, and gave my father the words that he would ever after try to live by, from Roger Bacon's Four Stumbling Blocks to Truth:

1. The influence of fragile or unworthy authority.
2. Custom.
3. The imperfection of undisciplined senses.
4. Concealment of ignorance by ostentation of seeming wisdom.

Over the years, he often invoked this mantra at the family dinner table, and when he died, I had it copied by a calligrapher for my daughter and son and my brother's two girls. But I think he would have left the *Father's Message* blank, no matter what wisdom came to mind, confident that my mother was giving me all I needed to find my true north.

Did she have an inkling of how those nine little words would bedevil me? Not in my meanest, maddest moment have I thought so. I picture a softening of her determined jaw, a half-smile on her lips, as she bent over the pink page, a fountain pen in her artist's hand: a severely disciplined woman daring to hope. With the best Will in the world, she would save me from the sort of folly that had been her undoing.

It was all about Stalin; has to have been. He broke her heart in 1939, when he signed the infamous nonaggression pact with Hitler. If only she'd been true to herself, she would have seen the lie at the heart of Communism: That's what her *Mother's Message* meant. Here was an inoculation as crucial as any the doctor would give me. Her little girl would grow up tyrant-proof.

You might say the shot took. I've been involved in some of the political struggles of my day, but I never signed over my soul, never stopped doubting and asking questions. I cry for joy in the voting booth, and even as I'm soaking my Kleenex, I wonder when the bucket of cold water will come. I owe Caroline that skepticism. The one tyrant she couldn't save me from was herself. My mother, my Stalin.

From childhood forever onward, she deemed me true to myself only when I was true to her. "The apple doesn't fall far from the tree," she must have said a thousand times—this unpious, untrite woman who read Ezra Pound and e. e. cummings, who upbraided my fifth-grade teacher for promulgating Edgar Guest.

I got carsick and seasick and airsick, and she welcomed my misery as proof that I was made of her. I had trouble with biology in high school, and she cheered the synchrony of our minds, more gratified by my teacher's despair than if I'd brought home an A. Biology had been her worst subject. The sciences weren't for *us*. When it came time to choose a college, I applied "early decision" to Sarah Lawrence for two reasons: My mother's parents couldn't afford it in the Depression years, and it had no science or math requirement. Who knew I'd grow up to write, inter alia, fantastical medical fiction, empowered by my ignorance of science, but eternally yearning for it?

Wandering back through my life, I see example after example of my beloved Stalin's hegemony, especially in the early teen years, when one's sense of self is so fragile. If I just overcame my revulsion to the country club life, I, too, might be a champion golfer; everyone said I had her swing. I only *thought* I wanted to wear ballet skirts; really, I wanted to sport the tailored tweed that *she* wore with grace. Then again, when I hit puberty, Mother assured me that I would have easy pregnancies, because she had; and, years later, it was so—perhaps in great part because I believed her.

In my childhood bedroom, I had plenty of mirrors. My maple dresser had a matching triptych mirror (great: I could see my nose in profile). The outside of my closet door had a grown-up full-length mirror, the envy of my friends. Every bedroom in our home had such a mirror; my father's father was a glazier, and my parents liked giving him business. And from my maternal grandfather came a piece of furniture so remarkable that I have it still: an Alice in Wonderland dressing table, with Tweedledee and Tweedledum forming the base, and turrets on either side of the oval looking glass.

I peered at my image for hours, waiting for revelation that never came. Whatever I saw had pale substance next to my mother's judgment. And not just my mother's. I grew up in West Hartford, Connecticut; and in that place, at that time, the phone would ring with reviews of my appearance after a country club cookout or some other event of national importance. My mother would deliver the judgments with suitable gravity. "Joy said your hair looked adorable, but how could I let you go out in that unflattering dress?"

More than fifty years ago, and I remember the dress. I'd just discovered Fitzgerald, and here was a dropped-waist number right out of "Bernice Bobs Her Hair"—red and white gingham, with a kicky white flounce at the hem. If I saw it today, I would buy it, madly missing my mother, even missing Joy, whose daughters wore pastel.

Whose self is it, anyway? Every parent and child—but I think, especially, every mother and daughter—has to duke out that one.

In "The Lost Children," Randall Jarell's perfect poem of parenthood and boundaries, he defines a mother as the "authority" on her child . . . and the necessary loss of that awesome status as a child grows in self-awareness, self-definition. I know from both sides now how delicious and dangerous it is to have a daughter who so resembles you that strangers feel impelled to remark on the likeness, as if you might have missed it. Lucky for her psyche and her looks, my own daughter, a quirky beauty, also resembles her father. Mostly, she looks like herself.

Growing up, I wanted to look like my father because I wanted to be like him. Physically, and every other way, I could be only a failed version of my mother, put together more elegantly than I (those legs! and she could walk in high heels, while I am awkward even in flats) and far more faithful to herself as a painter than I've been to myself as a writer. But she wouldn't allow it. My first passport, when I was seventeen, noted that my eyes were blue, like hers. I just checked in the True Mirror: they're hazel, like my father's. Eyes do change color, even in adulthood. You can look it up. But was I really a blue-eyed girl? Or was it just that my mother saw me so— and thus my mirror did?

I got even, as she loved to say. God, did I get even. I came to a passionate belief that nothing was more specious and destructive than the notion that each of us has a true self. "To thine own selves be true" was my very obsessive motto. At thirty-one, I put an ad in the *Village Voice*, seeking a stranger with whom to test the thesis that each of us contains the seeds of many beings. I loved everyone who answered the ad but easily chose a Marxist feminist bisexual psychologist, married on weekends, who said, "I don't know whether to have my wisdom teeth out now or wait until the swap and let you have them out." She got it! We spent three months trading details and prepping our friends, so that when we traded keys to each other's apartments we would also trade our selves: beliefs, ideas, passions, even her taste for plain yogurt and mine for Irish whiskey. My first nonfiction book, *The Life Swap*, recounts the adventures and misadventures that rolled out. It actually happened: I did my best to become Micki with an open marriage, while she was (supposedly) trying to be a swinging single straight writer: me. Yes, I slept with her husband and her young male lover (who felt like *my* husband and lover, though I'd never laid eyes on them before); I was gay on Wednesday night. I not only ate but enjoyed the dreaded plain yogurt; in Micki's memory, I still eat it every day.

Maybe that's how we were in 1973. Maybe the truly stunning thing is that my parents went along with the swap, took part in the theatrics, when they couldn't talk me out of it. They actually welcomed Micki into my childhood home as if she were their daughter. Afterward, when I polled the participants for contributions to the book, my mother wrote a witty, scolding, but tender piece in defense of the one and only real Nancy. Still hers to define, but how could I mind?

The hazel-eyed woman I see in the True Mirror is also my blue-eyed mother. And my father, my brother, my children— and even the woman with whom I swapped my life, though she wanted to change me, not be me. I think the secret of the mirror is that it's not a single surface. Two pieces of glass reflect each other, and somehow you know it. Yes, space-age glue makes the seam disappear, but that's not the wonder. The wonder is that it's there, an antidote to flatness, hinting at infinity.

My home is a trove of mementos of my children's early years, but there are no baby books. I dreaded my own power over my kids. I so didn't want to be Stalin. But I've always secretly wanted to write a nine-word *Mother's Message*, if only I knew what it was.

My daughter is thirty now and my son is twenty-four. They are brilliantly their own people, the authorities on themselves—*worth*y authorities, I think my father would say. And at last I know what I want to tell them.

You can't look into the same mirror twice. You . . .

NANCY WEBER is the author of a memoir, *The Life Swap*, and the novels *The Playgroup* and *Brokenhearted*. She worked with composer Alexander Zhurbin to adapt the lyrics of *Seagull: The Musical*, which had a reading at the 2005 New York Musical Theatre Festival and is in development. Mother of two grown children, she holds degrees from Sarah Lawrence and the French Culinary Institute. She owns a catering business called Between Books She Cooks. Her next book is a sequel to *The Playgroup*. She chairs two not-for-profit agencies: FROST'D, serving people at risk for HIV/AIDS, and National Music Theater Network (NMTN).

VICKI TOPAZ

LITTLE MISS SOMEBODY

Victoria Zackheim

When I was eight years old, a third-grader, my life was filled with music—singing, piano lessons, tap dancing (unlike my talented best friend, Barbara, mine was perhaps the worst performance ever of "I Am a Little Dutch Girl"), and a home in which I was taught to love everything from Yma Sumac to Puccini, Miriam Makeba to the Weavers. I was thrilled when I was finally old enough to audition for the school chorus. My voice was sweet and sure, my pitch accurate, and I sang for the music director with joy and

185

confidence. When I finished my song, the elderly woman with long braids twisted atop her head pulled me aside and offered an explanation that went something like, "You have a lovely voice, dear, but I'm sure your parents would never allow you to sing in the Christmas program, so it's better if you don't join our little group." I didn't understand that she was making reference to our being Jewish, yet I still recall the humiliation, deep and long-lasting. Despite my passion for music and singing, I never again auditioned for a choral group.

What was so magical about a choir? I saw it as a way to belong, to fit in, which was something I desperately wanted. Being reared by socially conscious, red-diaper-baby parents in a south-central Los Angeles town with a large African American population—all of whom lived on the other side of the tracks—I was taught early on to fight for what I believed. (Actually, to fight for what my parents believed because, as children, how can we really understand?) In those days, the fight was civil rights in a world with too many wrongs. Whenever I voiced my opinion, whether as a child of seven or seventeen, I managed to create hostility among quite a few classmates and teachers. I tried to balance this by winning over friends, but my attempts were too obvious and resulted in even greater isolation.

By the time I hit puberty, I had no idea who I was, or where I belonged in the complicated map of my life. In truth, I could barely look at myself in the mirror, because the face staring back was that of a lonely child who tried too hard to be liked and accepted. I never went along with the crowd when the comments became racist, so the more fervent my argument, the greater my sense of loneliness.

I was a naive girl whose path was supposed to take her first into education and then, if my father got his not-so-secret wish, to social reform and perhaps elected public office. My own secret wishes were more dramatic: I wanted to be a singer and a doctor. (Looking back, I now see that had anyone asked me what I wanted to be, I would have said, "Anyone but my parents," which probably didn't make me different than most teenagers.) How could I have known that I would grow into a cautious young woman afraid to expose too much, a woman who would sometimes feel as if she had thrown herself under a train . . . or wished she could?

Throughout my teenage years, the girl in that mirror became defined more by the expectations of her parents and teachers than by her own. Despite my earlier humiliation, I continued singing, but never in a group. (Unless you count my early duets with Patricia, standing together at the microphone set up in the Theodore Roosevelt Elementary School cafeteria, where unsuspecting children trying to eat their lunches were heartily serenaded.)

Always the wishful girl, I learned the words to nearly every Broadway musical from the forties, fifties, and then the sixties, my fantasy being to burst onto the music scene and be quickly discovered. Other than that loathsome choir director, was there any reason why Yul Brynner shouldn't dance *me* around a stage made to resemble a palace in Siam? And was it so far-fetched to imagine *me* attached to a wire and sailing out over the audience, while singing *I'm flying! Look at me, way up high, suddenly here am I, I'm flying!* in my most adorable Peter Pan voice?

With music on the brain, I was nevertheless heading toward that tried-and-true career path followed by respectable young women: teaching. As a toddler, I had suffered from, and then been surgically relieved of, a hearing loss that facilitated communication with the deaf students who participated in a special program in our public school. Therefore, I was not only expected to teach, but to teach the deaf. In my senior year, my science requirement was waived so I could assist in an English class for hearing-handicapped sophomores. It was not until the following year that I understood how this "honor" would prove to be the worst academic choice ever made on my behalf. But that's getting ahead of the story.

No matter how often I was reminded that teaching was a respectable profession, or what an excellent fall-back career it would be (as if the husband I had yet to meet had already died and/or left me penniless), I did not want to teach. I wanted something more colorful, more dramatic. At the very least, more . . . different. Being a kid, I had no idea what *different* looked like. Since my family and teachers agreed that I would be a special ed. teacher, I plodded on, but my inner yearnings traveled in other directions. If I did my internship at Columbia or the Albert Einstein School of Medicine, then I could be available whenever auditions were announced. Secret passions are the right of every child. (Perhaps not so secret, because I can still hear my father knocking on the bathroom door and reminding me that if I insisted on singing the entire score of *West Side Story* in the shower, there would be no hot water left for him.)

I wonder why so many of our youthful ambitions are held in secret. That was certainly true for me, and I expect it is true for many. In my case, I had developed my own personal and highly classified A-to-Z list of what I needed to accomplish in order to be *somebody*. Not necessarily somebody famous (or infamous, for that matter), but *somebody*. And if I couldn't cross off more than a few of those needs, I had failed.

My mother had been seriously ill for years, so I did what dutiful daughters were supposed to do—without the good-natured smiles—and rarely made waves. I learned early on not so much to push aside my doubts and discontents as to hide them, even from myself. I was, in a sense, the personification of Goody Two-Shoes. Case in point: I felt sorry for a boy who asked me out several times, so I agreed to let him take me to a drive-in movie, where he proceeded to pout through the first film because I wouldn't let him kiss me. I fell asleep during the second film and felt so guilty I agreed to one kiss. That one short—and may I add disgustingly sloppy—smooch resulted in missing school for a month while I recovered from mononucleosis. (When I asked him later if he had ever had it, he smiled and said, "Yes, and it's nearly gone!") That should have been a lesson, wouldn't you think? And yet my need to please continued to flow like a raging river seeking inlets of calm.

I was accepted into the University of California at Berkeley, got my dorm assignment, and imagined a banner reading *Flight to Freedom!* waving on the front lawn of our house. Due to my mother's health, however, my parents asked me to attend UCLA, where I could live on campus and still be within reach. Looking back, I can't imagine how my proximity could have made them feel better. I was a sullen teenager, moping about and, like so many girls of seventeen, more than ready to leave home. I would have thought they wanted some real distance from me. Hell, *I* wanted some real distance from me!

Off I went to university, stunned by its city-size. It took me forever to find the office of my adviser. Arriving with great anticipation—in eight years, I would be a doctor!—the appointment did not go as planned. I recall a rather smarmy man who tapped his pencil against a manila folder bearing my name. He made little humming sounds as he extracted a sheet of paper. "I see you've listed pre-med as your major." I nodded, proud to be a teenager who knew where her life was going. "And yet you skipped high school chemistry." I explained about the special dispensation, but he was not impressed. He took a long time to scan a short list and his frown increased. "In your first semester, you'll need to take organic chemistry, for which you are absolutely not qualified, as well as German and English IA, plus something in the social sciences—I recommend anthropology—and a course in the arts." And then he smiled. His teeth were tobacco-stained, giving him a predatory look. No need to glance around to find his prey.

That's when I became an English major, with a minor in speech. It wasn't that I didn't love the idea of taking on that challenge, of clawing my way through those courses and foisting myself on the medical establishment; it was that I was terrified. Somehow, even at seventeen, I understood that it was not the establishment on which I would be hoisting myself, but my own petard. As sophisticated as I yearned to be, I was still a child and felt quite illiterate when compared to the students in my dormitory, some of them grown women who went to class dressed in two-piece suits and pumps. I had always been an avid reader, so how difficult could an English major be? And having won, or come close to winning, local, regional, and state speech tournaments, I was sure I could swing that speech minor. I caved in on the spot and dumped the dream of medicine. Feeling quite defeated, I performed a desperate act of academic defiance and, turning my back on four years of high school Spanish, in which I was nearly fluent, signed up for Italian. So like me to do things the hard way.

At university, I learned some things about studying (it was a good idea to try it on occasion) and enjoyed my first experiences with anonymity (no one cared *what* classes I took, career I pursued, or the politics of my parents). I also discovered that I could cut class. With 650 students in my psych lecture, attendance was not recorded. Nor did anyone notice that, in my 8 a.m. Italian class, I frequently showed up in a trench coat covering my nightgown. For me, that was beyond bold . . . it was outright madcap.

I took two semesters of musical comedy and loved it. One of my classmates, Bonnie Franklin, went on to Broadway and a star role in *Applause*, while I humbly enrolled in Introduction to Acting for nonmajors. I was both thrilled and terrified when I was cast in one of the year-end one-act plays. I soon learned that I got the role not because I could act, but because I could sing and play the guitar. There were extensive rehearsals—was it my imagination, or did the director/playwright gnash his teeth whenever I read my lines? We had one performance, and I was terrible, self-conscious and surprisingly timid. Today, I can laugh about naively assuming that, being the only nontheater major student to get a role, I would naturally earn an excellent grade. When the grade arrived and it was a C, the sting of failure morphed into palpable humiliation. My leading man, John Rubenstein, would go on to Broadway and *Pippin*, while I would perform a community service and disappear into acting obscurity.

Theater disgrace aside, university life was rarely dull. In no particular order, this is how my future unfolded: I reveled in my freedom, learned how to play bridge and shoot a very respectable game of pool, went on academic probation, pulled it together, got arrested for being armed with a deadly weapon (maybe I'll write that memoir after all), fell in love with a very sweet boy (we were both nineteen), nearly flunked out, switched my major to speech so I could graduate with my dignity intact, married after my junior year, miraculously graduated, moved to San Francisco, went to graduate school (yes, a master's in special education/speech pathology: I was a very good daughter), had two exquisite children (a boy and then a girl, as required), and then glanced in the mirror one day, around age thirty-five, and did not recognize the woman staring back.

What happened to that girl who was promised she could

achieve anything and everything? I had no idea if I had fulfilled my family's dreams, but I was absolutely certain that I was a dismal failure when it came to fulfilling my own. My life had evolved into an ongoing string of "busy work" that included slicing and bagging copious supplies of oranges for soccer games and unending carpools. (One year I realized I was doing thirteen carpool turns a week and enjoyed a fleeting fantasy of running away.) I sat on the boards of various community organizations and made appearances with my husband at his professional and philanthropic events. While some wives are able to perfect the art of smiling graciously, I was not. Instead, I had in some ways reverted back to my surly adolescent moue, much to my husband's displeasure and my own chagrin. If I felt put upon, forced to be somewhere and someone I did not want to be, most attempts to mask my discontent failed miserably. I could no more pretend to be a willing participant than I could hide the deep disappointment I felt about the direction my life had taken. This was not so much about marriage or motherhood, but about fulfillment and purpose. My children were beautiful, healthy, smart, funny. The problem was their mother, a woman who was starved for creativity, for that elusive satisfaction so many of us struggle to achieve. In my case, neither fulfillment nor purpose was anywhere to be found. Like Gertrude Stein's reference to her hometown of Oakland, thus was my view of myself: There was no there there.

I think of those times—preparing for college, choosing the one I would attend, marriage at twenty, the roles I played as wife—and realize that, in so many ways, I was too often at the mercy of other people's decisions about my life. Or, at the least, I felt that I was.

After fifteen years, my marriage failed.

The thing about being a divorced woman of thirty-five is that one has the opportunity to begin a new life in an entirely new way. With absolutely no interest in pursuing my career in speech pathology, I turned to writing. I needed to earn a living, so I found a mentor who guided me into advertising and then hired me to be a junior copywriter. The agency's head writer was soon fired, the second in command quit, and there I was, the only writer and loving it. Dull corporate brochures were bearable, knowing there was a radio or television commercial just around the corner. When I left the agency to become a free-lance writer, there was more work than I could handle. It was the eighties and Silicon Valley was producing life-changing products at mach speed. I discovered that my gift was the ability to write reader-friendly technical ads, brochures, and videos about products that completely baffled me. Like so many elements of my life, I could string concepts together into a cohesive message without comprehending its content.

The most enjoyable part of being a freelance writer is the opportunity to write for all kinds of clients. I joined a team of political writers dedicated to the election of Democratic candi-dates and loved that I was actually paid to combine my love of politics with my love of words. From mail pieces (we called them "hit pieces" because they were attack-oriented) to radio spots, position papers to campaign speeches, the work was exciting and fulfilling. When I was hired to write the stump speeches for the senior member of the United States Senate, I felt as if I had arrived, as if I had finally become that woman I wanted to be. The senator and I were introduced several times, but he never remembered having met me. The biggest assign-ment of my professional life and I was invisible.

The election ended, my children went off to university, and I spent five years in Paris trying to figure out where my heart would take me next. It was in that exquisite city, living alone and creating an entirely new life, a new existence, that I began to confront myself. How could I have been so naive as to believe that finding a profession I loved meant I had found myself? There was no doubt that I needed to pursue an entirely different path and open myself to discoveries based on reality—not hopefulness or even avoidance—but the going would be far more difficult than I had imagined.

Looking back, I'm convinced these discoveries could never have taken place had I not separated myself from family and community. The very act of learning to be completely alone and relying only on myself proved to be the greatest learning experience of my life.

Fast-forward fifteen years. My children are adults, successful in their professions, married to loving and supportive spouses who encourage them to follow their paths. Not much parenting is required from me these days, which is perhaps how it should be. But that's fine, because now there's something that fills me with such awe that I am barely able to contain my around-the-clock joy: grandchildren. Twin girls, and they live twenty minutes away. They call me Mima, and my daughter likes to point out that the girls have bestowed upon me the adulation and enthusiasm often given a rock star. This will change—they're only six, after all, so the magnet of parties and boys is a good while off—but for the time I am nurtured and sustained by their unconditional love. Not to say that I wouldn't be thrilled to meet a professorial, libidinous, single man, but even that cannot compare to the emotions evoked by these two little girls. Truly, how amazing is it to merely stretch out your arms and have at least one little person come flying into them? Heaven.

I never made it to Broadway, but I did experience the joy of publishing a novel, as well as selling two very well-received anthologies—and this one makes three—in the past three years. The first one got me on national television, my greatest accomplishment being that I made it through the entire segment of the *Today Show* without fulfilling a recurring nightmare that had to do with puking on the host. As it happened, Ann Curry was warm and gracious, and she put me immediately at ease.

The theme of the first book is infidelity, and I suddenly found myself the go-to woman for everything on the subject. Interviews, radio and television appearances, newspaper and magazine articles, all that an author could dream and rarely achieve, and here it was, delivered to me on a beautiful platter. At first, I wondered how this could happen to a woman who had never been unfaithful, nor had suffered infidelity. As my grandmother used to say: just my luck. (Okay, she said this whenever a friend died, and I was never sure if she meant "luck" because it had been a friend and not her . . . or if it had some ironic meaning, like she wished she had been so lucky and had died instead. With Grandma, you never knew.) And it *was* luck, as it turned out, because that book opened the door to the second anthology, which is about body image, aging, and acceptance, and I certainly know plenty about those. In truth, if they passed out diplomas for matriculating in Body Image, Aging, and Acceptance, I'd have multiple PhDs and no doubt be invited to march in some processional wearing a long black cape and draped in the colors of the department.

I love the synchronicity of life, the way lessons seem to arrive when they're least expected and most needed. A few months ago, ten days before my son's wedding, while running out of my place to meet a friend—that new outfit I was taking to

New York the next day for the *Good Morning America* interview *had* to have a scarf, right?—I tripped and fell down my stairs. I remember being on the hardwood floor, unable to raise my head, and thinking, "Oh, shit." And then my daughter, her little girls, and my loving neighbor Roxann arrived, followed closely by the fire department and the ambulance, and off I went to the trauma unit at San Francisco General. The swellings and bruises healed quite well, but the loss of memory from the concussion was unsettling. Not devastating, because I knew I'd recover—I made it to the wedding, my shiner hidden nicely behind makeup—but it gave me a taste of what might come should I, like my grandmothers (and in another year, my mother), live into my nineties.

What sustained me over the following month was the outpouring of love and support I received from family and friends. Rides to the market, surprise visits with flowers, e-mails checking on my recovery, phone calls from friends who insisted I stay on the line and talk, communicate, so they could push me to remember words and phrases that would not come: the title of my novel, what I'd eaten for breakfast that morning.

No need to be a genius to understand that publishing books and being interviewed by the media is nice, but being loved and being healthy are what it's all about.

I thought I'd become more poetic as I aged, more philosophical and even mysterious. But something amazing happened when I hit sixty: although it took six decades, I finally understood that being a *somebody* is not the opposite of being a *nobody*. It is, in fact, being oneself.

I may not have fulfilled everyone else's expectations for me, but I do believe I have come close to fulfilling my own. I've always longed to be part of a community, and so I am. A community of friends, a community of writers, a global community of people who care about one another, whether we're acquainted or not.

Today, when I look in the mirror, I'm apt to notice first the water spots and toothpaste spatters on the glass. After that's cleaned away, I see a woman staring back who, despite—and yes, because of—her wrinkles, unmanageable mop of silver hair, and more weight than is good for her health or her self-image, is someone I've come to accept and for whom I feel a genuine fondness.

VICTORIA ZACKHEIM is the author of *The Bone Weaver* and editor of two other anthologies, *The Other Woman: 21 Wives, Lovers, and Others Talk Openly about Sex, Deception, Love, and Betrayal* (GrandCentral) and *For Keeps: Women Tell the Truth about Their Bodies, Growing Older, and Acceptance* (Seal Press). Zackheim is story developer and writer of the documentary film *Tracing Thalidomide: The Frances Kelsey Story*, now in development with On the Road Productions, writer of *More Than A Poet's Daughter: The Story of Ada Byron Lovelace* (On the Road Productions), and coproducer and writer of the documentary *When G.I. Joe Is a Muslim* (On the Road Productions). Victoria teaches in the UCLA Extension Writers' Program and writes/records commentaries for the *Mimi Geerges Show*, XM-Satellite and public radio. Her Web site is http://www.victoriazackheim.com.

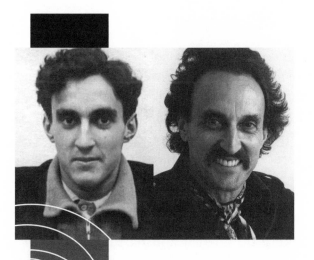

LIFE SENTENCE

Leon Whiteson

W ay back when, I see a scruffy school-
boy in the British colony of Southern
Rhodesia (now Zimbabwe) entering his home
city's main public library for the very first time.
He lives in a house with few books, apart from
a religious tome or two and the trashy romance
novels his mother devours, and the library's
gray stone portals seem like gates guarding a
trove of maybe risky knowledge.

In the early 1940s, my homeland was a
sleepy region in the warm African interior, and
I was a young Rip Van Winkle, long snug in

199

my country's slumber—a drowsiness so deep that even the world war raging across the northern hemisphere seemed hardly more than distant thunder. In my early teens, though, I began to be troubled by a premonition that it was time to wake up, that it might be foolish to go on dreaming.

Half a century before, in Kiev, my Russian Jewish grandfather, Matthew Weitzen, bought a ticket to New York City. After a long, slow odyssey across Europe, he finally hustled his wife and six kids up a gangway in Southampton—onto the wrong boat. He spoke little English and hated asking directions. Ten days later, the Weitzen brood—renamed Whiteson on their travel documents by some offhand British official—landed in Cape Town rather than Manhattan. My grandpa never quite comprehended his error. Had spiteful goyim hidden the Statue of Liberty? Compounding his confusion, Matthew trekked north in the 1890s to raw new territories north of the Limpopo, recently appropriated for the British Empire by Cecil John Rhodes, and settled in a city of tents named Bulawayo, which was Ndebele for *site of slaughter*. All his life he wondered how on earth a *gute mensch* like himself had ended up in this *nothing place* among strangers black and white, on a far edge of civilization. Africa, he declared, "*ist nicht gemacht fur ein Yid*," not made for a Jew. In 1902, Conrad published *Heart of Darkness*, voicing an even more drastic European ambivalence about Africa.

In the year following my bar mitzvah, Grandpa Matt's feeling of being out of place had also begun to bother me, sparking an unease that was something more than the awkwardness of adolescence. Was I African or European? Did my future really lie under the bright skies of the casually racist Rip Van Winkleland where I was born and raised? Then again, what was Europe, apart from the old man's bitterly remembered, pogrom-riddled homeland, or the abstract territory represented by a map in my schoolroom, dotted with colored pins to mark the conflict of vast Second World War armies? Yet, until that particular midsummer's day, it had never occurred to me that the public library might offer some insight into my growing disquiet. I'd often cycled past the solemn structure and its screen of dusty jacaranda trees without really noticing it. Suddenly, I felt impelled to enter the building. Heart thumping, I jumped off my bike and ran inside. After the street's glare, the airy reading room was cool and dark. Ramparts of books rose up on all sides, exuding a musky aroma, a dangerous, somehow sexual smell that gave me goosebumps. The snooty librarian behind the desk shot me a sharp glance, noting my gawky limbs, floppy khaki shorts, crooked school tie, sweat-soiled hat, and sagging socks. I shuffled, awkward as a heathen in a temple, sure her priestess eye divined my ignorance. To escape her scrutiny, I plunged into the stacks. A book slid into my hand, as if by its own volition. The title on its cracked leather binding made me tremble: *Crime and Punishment*.

A page fell open at random, sucking me into the labyrinth of dim alleyways where Raskolnikov writhed on his bed of rags, tortured by remorse for murdering the old hag of a moneylender. In this ambiance—erotic with despair, charged with fertile terror and thrilling mystery—I heard echoes of my secret, guilty soul that somehow suspected the world was more fascinating, complex, and fraught than everyone around me— family, teachers, leaders—would acknowledge. Like a junkie hot for the next fix, I gulped down all of Dostoevsky, jumping to Gogol, Goncharov, Turgenev, Tolstoy, Bulgakov, and Babel. Adrift in the stacks, my soft young mind was bent out of shape between my familiar, yet suddenly alien, reality, and a new old world, fantastical yet profoundly real.

My heart leapt to my throat when Dmitri Karamazov, accused murderer and self-proclaimed *lowest reptile*, cries out from his prison cell: "I think I could stand anything, any suffering, only to be able to repeat to myself every moment, 'I exist.'"

I exist!

The cry rang in my head. Could I really "stand anything, any suffering," to claim my own true country of the mind, my personal *Heart of Darkness*?

One thing was sure: words had led me into this provocative confusion, and so they must hold the key to some kind of resolution. Somewhere in the maze of pages read and yet-to-be-read, written and yet-to-be-written, was hidden my own vital life sentence—one that begins, *I exist . . .*

Flash-forward through decades of restless peregrination; years living successively in South Africa, England, Spain, Greece, Canada, and, finally, Los Angeles. Along the way, I abandon my original profession as an architect, seduced by the compulsion called writing, the search for that life sentence. Along the way, I end one long marriage and start another, help to raise a son and a daughter, publish novels, write plays for the BBC, and become an architecture critic for several newspapers and magazines in order to earn a living while I scribble.

My first marriage was rocky from the get-go. In my freshman year at architecture school in Cape Town, I met a sexy, moody twenty-one-year-old art student. The first woman I slept with, she soon became pregnant. I lacked the moral courage and sophistication to cry out, "No, I don't want this!" So, at nineteen, I was daddy to George,* and a few years later to Sophia.* I often wondered why she had chosen a callow man-boy like me to make her happy. Frankly, I was desperate,

---

*pseudonym

and in those student years there were times when I walked on parapets half hoping to fall off.

On my better days, I tried to convince myself that my marriage was a negative apprenticeship, a long, hard lesson in how not to be with a woman. On bad days, I fell into a trough of cheap cynicism about the hopelessness of any emotional attachment. On my very worst days, I was overwhelmed by the fear that I was incapable of loving anyone, other than my children. I began to wonder if I really existed at all. But willy-nilly I'd taken on the responsibility of becoming a husband and father, and there was no other honorable way forward than to stiffen my spine and grow up fast.

The moment I got my degree, I insisted we leave for England. In the early 1950s, the cruelly absurd situation in South Africa under apartheid was getting worse by the week, to the point where you had to either dedicate your life to combating a petty, vicious regime or get the hell out, and my choice was clear. As the ship left Cape Town harbor, I looked at the trio of mountains ringing the bay—Table Mountain, Lion's Head, and Devil's Peak—and tried to imagine Grandpa Matt's feelings at first sight of his new continent. "*Nkosi sikele iAfrika . . .*" I murmured. God save Africa—but without me. As the ship rolled on through gray Atlantic wastes, I spent hours leaning on the rail, sucking in salt air, savoring the sense of hovering between past and future. I was wild with expectation; anything seemed possible in the wide, forthcoming world.

Desdemona,* already pregnant with Sophia, was seasick for most of the ten days it took the Union Castle liner to travel to Southampton; she spent much of the journey lying on her bunk, face to the wall. Too delighted to be getting away, I ignored her sorrows. *Out of Africa!* In my mind the phrase had a resonance quite unlike Isak Dinesen's.

---

*pseudonym

For a raw colonial youth, London was the heart of Empire; the very name was magical. And it was snowing when we came out of London's Waterloo Station, the first snow three-year-old George and I had ever seen. Spontaneously, we rolled around in the soft white stuff, shouting for joy. Altogether, the sheer pleasure of being in England was exhilarating, even down to the damp days and foggy nights, the somber buildings and the glum streets filled with shabby folk scuttling this way and that in the postwar austerity. After long rambles through the West End's parks and squares, I liked to linger on the stone embankment in Westminster and watch fat barges waddle through the Thames's muddy stream, enjoying the pulse of a powerful *world city*. I went to work for the London County Council, designing public housing to replace the East End slums damaged by wartime bombing, helping rebuild a proud country I could love.

However, within a year or two after landing in England, that early delight began to fade. There was a big worm in the English apple, I found. It seemed that the English, for all their fortitude, had no sense of how dangerous it is to be human. Despite the still-evident horrors of the Blitz, Londoners behaved as if such recent furies were an aberration. I could rationalize the obtuseness of this attitude, and even admire it, but it began to disturb me more and more. Also, I was irritated by the Englishman's fascination with the intricacies of his elaborate caste system. Slight nuances of accent, education, and manners were obsessively remarked and mocked, as if each person's sense of worth depended on knowing exactly where he stood in the pecking order. In their essential meanness, such gradations seemed even more futile than the harsh racial rankings of South Africa. Anyway, outsiders like me were tolerated but irrelevant. When I wasn't condescended to as a colonial, I was none-too-politely pegged as a member of the Hebrew persuasion. Once again, I was a familiar stranger.

My growing uneasiness was compounded by doubts about the kind of architecture I was so eagerly engaged in. It was a basic tenet of 1950s modernism that architecture was a means to craft a better world. The credo was simple, and simple-minded: improve the environment in which people lived, worked, and played, and society would surely progress. This utopian ambition was expressed in a bleak, *functional* building style. But the working-class tenants whose lives we were hoping to *improve* hated the host of towering apartment blocks we created in our futuristic fervor. In such high-rise hells, moms could only peer down anxiously upon the pinpoint heads of their kids playing in scraggly parks far below. Dads, depressed by the anonymity of these arid new neighborhoods, lingered in the pubs. It was all very distressing, for once a designer's faith is corrupted by uncertainty, his whole rationale begins to crumble.

Also, the blurry English countryside lacked the resonance of the veld, with its sharp divisions between earth and sky. In the English mist, I yearned for Africa's clarities.

Then I discovered the Mediterranean.

My first sight of that glorious sea was a revelation. The crispness in the air, the brilliance of the light, the terra-cotta tones of the terrain; the milky, blue-white canopy of air appeared as fresh as the dawn of creation. The towns and villages seemed to grow out of the ground like an organic musculature stretched over the earth's rough brown ribs. By contrast, England's green and pleasant land was too tamed, too made over in the Englishman's image—one I could never make mine.

A few years later, Desdemona, the children, and I went to live in Spain. In Spain, and later, in Greece, I was simply *extranjero* or *xenos*, stranger, and glad of it; there's a simplicity in clearly not belonging. In the Villa Santa Ana, in the town of Altea south of Alicante, I began to write. My time as an architect was over, for all sorts of reasons. Apart from my general ambivalence about architecture, I preferred being transported by the singular fluency of language to struggling with the sluggishness of concrete. Always those slippery sentences . . .

And then there was the marriage. Against all odds, it tottered on for two decades, kept going by our shared parental duty; a grinding, loveless era that seemed to last forever. Finally, the kids grew up and, one glum morning back in London, Desdemona and I separated.

It happened abruptly and ludicrously. Desdemona was fussy about her breakfast toast. She insisted it be made from a special organic bread named Nutty Compost, and that particular morning I'd lazily tried to pass off a substitute. She took one bite, grimaced in disgust, and threw the fake on the floor. "This is *not* Nutty Compost!" she shouted. As the toast crumbled on the tiles, so did our marriage.

I was troubled by the impact of our divorce on George and Sophia. I feared the damage we had done them by our unloving example could well last a lifetime. But to my surprise, neither of them seemed particularly upset. When I visited Sophia at Cambridge, where she was working on an undergraduate English degree, she told me she was positively pleased Desdemona and I had separated. "Your thing was always a botch. You should never have gotten together in the first place," she said. Her comment staggered me. Had our children always been aware of the essential impossibility of our marriage? But then, they were well placed to know.

As we strolled around the quad at Newnham College, I was proud of the handsome young woman at my side. I was struck by her resemblance to Desdemona at her age: the same abundance of dark brown hair; the same coal black eyes; the same sulky-sensual expression. We moved beyond the college grounds and across Kings, making our way toward the river. On the late spring day the sun was soft on the willows that drooped over the Cam, buttering the trailing leaves with yellow light. We sat on a grassy bank near the water and watched the occasional punt go by.

"I often wondered why you didn't just buzz off into the blue, on your own or with another woman," Sophia said. "Foolishly, you persisted. I never could, and never will."

Her words chilled me. They implied that the main lesson she had learned from observing our marriage was to be wary. "You have to love someone," I said. "'Love one another or die . . .'"

"Didn't Auden amend that to, 'Love one another and die'?" she retorted.

"I prefer the earlier version."

"You're sentimental," she accused. "Underneath all the disappointments and evasions, you still think it's possible to be human."

"What's the alternative?"

"Whatever gets you through the day. As the poet said, 'Everyone has the right to go to hell in his own way.'"

Her words hung in the air, little balloons of truth. I couldn't argue with them, but I hoped I wouldn't be forever condemned to my own half-chosen hell, or worse—a limbo of not quite existing. One thing I knew for certain: to escape such hard time, I'd need the help of the gods, plus a lot of luck.

Miraculously, I had such luck, and soon. Not long after Desdemona and I separated, I encountered Aviva and fell in love for the first time in my life.

I met her one summer in the town of Methymna, on the Greek island of Lesbos. I'd gone to that quiet place to write a novel about a burnt-out Rhodesian who returns to Bulawayo to help African rebels during their struggle for independence. By engaging in such radical action, my white hero hopes to purge his guilt and perhaps validate his existence. I put the work aside to focus on Aviva. Her heat warmed my frozen heart, melting the ice of its long winter. Altogether, the astonishment of loving staggered me; I felt like a Neanderthal discovering fire. After all, maybe I really did exist! And as a lover, of all things . . .

To think of myself as a lover wasn't easy, for many reasons. To start with, Lover was my mother Rebecca's edgy pet name for Charles, my father; his open, sometimes naked adoration often seemed to irritate her. "Your dad's a softie," she told me, and her tone implied a fatal weakness in his nature, especially in his submission to her iron will. Right up until her early death from Parkinson's disease, my mother never overcame her ambivalence about my father's fondness. Taking a cue from her, I tended to despise my dad, especially during adolescence, when I was struggling to find my own male way in the world. So I was startled to be overwhelmed by a passionate tenderness that was much like his—a wonderful, loving weakness. In belated atonement for my youthful rudeness, I wrote him a letter telling him I loved him and how much he meant to me. His reply was brief and sublimely matter-of-fact: "Of course you love me, my boy. I'm your Dad."

My feeling for Aviva was so intense that I wasn't deterred by the fact that she was married and had a pubescent son. Her relationship with a Canadian poet was troubled, and her response to me was supercharged by her unhappiness. By the end of that summer she had decided to leave her husband. Young David came with her, and we made our own new family.

There've been many ups and downs in our marriage, provoked by our variously awkward temperaments, but the passion and affection run deep, holding fast through several changes of geography, from London to Toronto and finally Los Angeles—moves dictated by job offers and other practicalities of survival in a writer's life.

During the civil war that raged in Rhodesia in the 1970s, as the Africans struggled for independence, I phoned my father in Bulawayo to find out if he was safe. He was touched by my concern, but also untroubled. "If I don't watch TV, I don't know there's a war on," he said. In 1980, the whites finally gave up and handed over political power to Robert Mugabe; Rhodesia became Zimbabwe. In the light of Mugabe's subsequent misrule, some might say the Europeans should never have surrendered; but after centuries of colonial condescension, Africans had to develop their own destiny, for good or ill. After all, everyone has the right to go to hell in his own way. How many outright hells have Europeans and Americans put themselves through in search of their souls?

After Rhodesia's demise, my father and most of my relatives fled the country to South Africa, Australia, and Israel, leaving behind little but the family graves. In effect, the country of my birth ceased to exist: I might have once been a Rhodesian, but I would never be a Zimbabwean. I was now not only away from Africa, my Africa was away from me, vanished in the dust of the continent's unsettled history. Even if I wanted to, I could never go home again.

This blunt fact shook me more than I expected. We may move away from the territory of our childhood and choose to live anywhere but there in body and in spirit, yet all the same we expect the country to continue in our absence in some familiar form. After a mere ninety years of existence, Rhodesia ended, turning my boyhood into a fable set in a ghost world. Sometimes I feel a spasm of nostalgia for that foolish, sleepy colony, a bubble of willful ignorance that finally burst. After all, it is my native land.

Los Angeles has turned out to be the perfect place for my portable spirit to come to rest. On the one hand, there's the absence of any distinctive local vernacular: no fixed LA-speak, so to say, demanding conformity or defiance. To paraphrase Theodor Herzl's remark about pre-Israel Palestine, LA is for me a town with no tongue, for a tongue with no town. Then there's the city's fabled gift of radical self-invention. Think Walt reimagining his Montana hamlet as Disneyland, or utterly English Isherwood channeling Swami Vivekananda in the Palisades; *gemütlich* Billy Wilder's jazzy *Some Like It Hot* or Viennese Richard Neutra and Rudolph Schindler creating the iconic architecture of Southland Modernism; and York-shireman Hockney making *A Bigger Splash* in Malibu. None of them need warp an accent or inclination to the dictates of any established cultural canon. To the contrary, such familiar strangers reinvent LA, while reinventing themselves. As just one more familiar stranger among many, I've grown easy with the disorientation that has long been my disposition, certainly since the day I entered the Bulawayo Public Library.

In this bouncy ozonesphere, with its desert winds and Pacific breezes, its perfumed jasmine, musky jacaranda, and sun-baked chaparral, its skinny palms scrubbing the bowl of sky like busy toilet brushes, I am free to fashion my own script. Herein lies the rare genius loci of this remarkable metropolis, this Dream Factory of the World, whose bright fables entranced me in the dark of Bulawayo's Princess Bioscope cinema on many a hot afternoon. On this blank screen you may conjure any wonder, even yourself. Especially yourself.

Over the years, the country of the mind I've explored has been neither as dramatic as Dmitri Karamazov's, nor as redemptive—in the flesh, that is. On paper, however, my fic-tional characters are often driven to try and redeem their lives through one sort of drastic act or another. Though their redemptions invariably turn out to be faulted or incomplete, they discover some way to go on that keeps faith with their intuitions. In literature, as in life, we all seek to serve out a livable life sentence.

So now there's this grandfatherly face in the looking glass, shadowed by that long-ago boy searching for a way to be. Finally I can say: *Yes, kid, in my own peculiar way, I exist.*

Southern Rhodesia–born architect and writer **LEON WHITESON** is the author of *A Place Called Waco: A Survivor's Story, A Garden Story, A Terrible Beauty: The Positive Role of Violence in Culture, Life & Society, Dreams of a Weeping Woman,* and an impressive collection of books and articles on architecture. Leon is married to author Aviva Layton.

SALLY GALL—LAURIE

RICHARD TOON

RUNAWAYS

Laurie Stone

NINETEEN

I am nineteen and we are already married. We are already something with two heads. I'm at Barnard College. Bruce is in law school at NYU. It's late and snowing hard, and we go out. We have to walk in the snow. We are living on Seventh Avenue and Fourteenth Street in a bourgeois building called the Vermeer, one of a series of high-rise apartments named after painters, maybe in homage to the area's artistic heritage. We're on the edge of the Village, not

213

exactly at the party, so when we walk we head south and east, toward the Lower East Side, the bosom of Bohemia.

It's coming down hard, and it's very cold, and we have walked for miles, but we can't go home yet. The streets are beautiful and quiet. The cars are polar bears with golden eyes, gliding along uncertainly. Bruce's mustache, eyebrows, and the curls peeking out of his hood are frosted over. He keeps knocking off the snow. We can see our breath. We can see the future, and it looks like a blizzard in a glass globe. I am born, and in a jump cut I am sixteen and watching *Jules and Jim* and *Breathless* in the Bleecker Street Cinema, thinking, "I like this thing I don't understand." I will want to wear a striped shirt and sell the *Herald Tribune* on the streets of Paris and have sex with a thug who has a beautiful mouth, but I will marry Bruce. Years later, when I am sixty-two and he is sixty-four and we have not seen each other in thirty-three years, he will say on the phone that we were runaways, flying toward each other to belong somewhere. He will say, "I still see it."

It's 2:30 in the morning, and the only place to duck into is Ratner's on Second Avenue, open all the time. No matter when you sit down, an old waiter lumbers over with a basket of warm onion rolls and holds his green pad in readiness for your order, even though the menu is as long as the Guttenberg Bible and you have just opened it. I can smell the rolls. They are made of challah dough and packed densely with sauteed onions, like a pocket, and some onions on top are blackened. The inside is soft and creamy. You don't need butter, though you slather it on anyway, and the rolls are so good you don't want anything more, but they're free and you have to order something. The waiter is wearing a white shirt and a tired black vest, and his face is creased with an ironic smile because he knows he's wittier than you and he's been practicing his lines. I don't imagine I will ever wear a vest like that, but I will be wrong, and when I'm well past fifty I will don an outfit exactly like his, including a little black bow tie, and I will pass around hors d'oeuvres at the kinds of parties I've attended as a writer. I will be there as a waiter, feeling excited and ashamed because I don't know what comes next.

There are others at Ratner's. A couple like us, but older and sexier. She wears bright crimson lipstick, and her gums emerge like actors behind a curtain when she smiles. It's a goofy grin and winning. Her red hair is long and straight, not the rust of some redheads, there's a little purple in the mix, and it's swept this way and that, and I can see why men want her, why anyone would. At another table is a man who is talking. He's spouting off on philosophy or politics or both. It's 1966, and Bruce and I have marched against the war in Vietnam. Kate Millet is my teacher at Barnard, and we are reading Beckett and Genet and she is calling me Mrs. Zimmer in class, which makes me turn to see if Bruce's tiny mother has appeared, but Kate means me, and I feel ridiculous even though I am Bruce the way Cathy is Heathcliff. I don't remember everyone in Ratner's. It was forty-three years ago. But I see the man who is talking and who lives nearby, who knows things or sounds like he does, who draws people to him, or maybe Bruce and I do that with the thrill we feel in the moment. Everyone in the restaurant moves toward each other, and we make a party. We shove tables together, and the waiter doesn't mind. We order mushroom and barley soup because that's what you eat at Ratner's, and a platter of bagels and lox, and we share it. The snow is getting heavier, and we are giddy with the prospect of trudging home, miles away.

No one wants to leave. We tell each other stories about who we are or we don't have to. The man who talks has a thin build and short-cropped hair brushed forward. He wears wire-rimmed glasses and keeps his scarf draped loosely around his neck. There is a small hole at the elbow of his brown sweater. He is a book editor or a schoolteacher or a graduate student stuck on his dissertation. At four or so there is movement. I don't know how it happens, but we leave together, all these strangers, and we go to the apartment of the talking man—the smart man or the lonely man. He has a narrow East Village flat crammed with books, a mattress on the floor covered with an Indian cotton throw, dusty plants. He empties his cupboards and places food and drink on a table by a window that looks out on Third Street, where the cars are buried.

This is how I want life to be: sudden and generous. In Europe, Bruce and I will buy train tickets from Geneva to Paris, and in the station a handsome man named René Boquet* will approach us. This is really his name. He looks like Belmondo in *Breathless*, and he will say to us in softly accented, excellent English that if we cash in our tickets he will drive us to Paris for half the price. On the way, he will guide us through the gardens of Fontainebleau and deliver us to the city of light at dawn. And we say okay, exchanging "Are we crazy?" looks, followed by "What the hell?" shrugs. During a thunderstorm in Monaco, René deposits us in a bar while he gambles at a casino, and Bruce and I attempt to describe our situation to the men on stools—there are only men—who shoot rapid-fire French at us. When René returns, he is good to his word, and by the time we stumble groggily through the rose gardens of the fabulous palace of French kings, we have fallen in love with each other and René will find us a hotel in the Arab quarter that costs one dollar a night and he will present us with our first Paris meal, a dinner prepared by his girlfriend, Marianne, of roasted *pintade*, a bird I have never heard of, served with its forlorn head tucked against its shoulder, and stuffed with boursin cheese, which I will taste for the first time.

*pseudonym

In the apartment of the talking man, we drink wine and smoke pot. Maybe my first joint. The talking man says, "If you can love an ant, you can love a human being," and I think I should remember this, even though I don't love ants, and it's harder to love people, no? I sit beside the red-haired woman in order to inhale her experience. She has a space between her front teeth and wears gloves with fur cuffs. She has the slim good looks of an actress Gene Kelly would cast in one of his movies, Leslie Caron, let's say, in *An American in Paris*, who portrays a lovely, obliging slip with the gift of appearing a blur, a zero—a type invented so Kelly can know where he begins and ends. But it's 1966, and the next year Bruce and I will march in Washington against the war and hear Norman Mailer deliver the speech at the Pentagon he will chronicle in *Armies of the Night*. Kate will invite me to join NOW, the National Organization for Women, and I will hear Ti-Grace Atkinson, NOW's president, defend her visit to Valerie Solanis, who is in jail awaiting trial for shooting Andy Warhol. Ti-Grace will say it's an act of solidarity with a feminist, for Valerie is the author of *SCUM Manifesto*, SCUM standing for Society for Cutting Up Men. The red-haired woman is not what she might have appeared even a year or two earlier. She works for a photographer near Herald Square and goes out on shoots and is assembling her own portfolio. Her boyfriend is a drummer, and they have slid into Ratner's after one of his gigs. She is twenty-five, the same age as my sister, but Ellen is in New Jersey with no job and two kids. She says she is happy, and I don't know what she means.

In 1983, I will write a piece for the *Village Voice* about *Minor Characters*, a memoir by Joyce Johnson recalling an affair she had with Jack Kerouac when she was an eager young woman looking for a way to get to the party. I will evoke a memory of myself at eleven or twelve, trying to imagine my future: "There would be a house with grass around it. There would be a white picket fence around the house. There would be a married woman standing in the backyard, staring over the fence. I knew I would be unhappy. I knew I would not want to be there, but I imagined this future nonetheless."* In this piece, I compare my experience at Barnard with Joyce Johnson's, ten years before. Joyce wants to be a writer, but her professors are men who feel wounded to be teaching girls and sneeringly say that women can't write. Instead I find Kate, who steeps us in avant-garde literature and lectures to us passionately in her industrial-strength gray skirts and tidy bun, speaking in a fake British accent from a couple of years at Cambridge. She calls herself a sculptor and lives with her Japanese husband, Fumio, who is also an artist, in a house on Bowery and First Street that totters this way and that and doesn't have a single level plane. Kate says she likes my mind. Her beautiful mind likes my mind, and through the vapor on the medicine chest mirror I see the possibility of Kate.

It's maybe six by the time Bruce and I set off for our apartment. A few months before, my father has stood on the bare parquet floor and said he will cosign the lease if we get married. I think I'm too young, but I am not going to leave Bruce any time soon, maybe never if we can keep moving. Sex will divide us—sex, or the desire we feel to be in two places at the same time. But now I'm with Bruce—a great tall thing with Beatles hair, adopted and an only child. The sight of him looming over his pint-sized parents is something out of a Diane Arbus freaks exhibit. Next door to us lives Adele Mailer, the wife whom some years earlier Norman stabbed with a penknife, nearly piercing her heart and claiming that, if he hadn't, he would have gotten cancer from repressed rage. Adele has beautiful, dusty skin the color of a clay pot and per-

*"Memoirs Are Made of This," VLS, April 16, 1983

forms in plays at LaMama and Theater for the New City. We listen to each other's lives through our thin, common wall and throw parties together. Kate and Fumio eat Swedish meatballs and crudités at our table from Macy's, a gift from Bruce's parents. I wear frameless, lilac glasses cut in octagonal shapes. I want to be one of the slouchy, prickly girls Kate favors who jump on motorcycles and write poetry, but I'm too studious, too married, too Mrs. Zimmer at the end of the day.

As the sky turns rosy and the last giant flakes flutter down, Bruce and I walk home from the East Village and never see our friends of the night again.

SIXTY

I am sixty and at Yaddo, the artist colony in Saratoga Springs. It's my birthday, and Suzy, my photographer friend, says I have to stretch toward people I don't like. What do I have to lose? Really, I have nothing to lose. Suzy says don't try, don't exert your will, just play through. At breakfast I sit with a man and woman I usually avoid. They're careful, giving away nothing of their real feelings. It's as if Charlie Rose can hear them in Manhattan and their writing futures depend on maintaining an inscrutable front. They scare me and piss me off. Their careers are going better than mine. Maybe they are just unencumbered by opinions. I smile and listen, and today their remarks sound like koans you could embroider on a pillow: "Writing leads to more writing," "Gravity is a force not well understood." Strangely, I feel lighter.

I will pretty much go anywhere to leave New York. Two thirty-five-story condos are going up outside my apartment, and I can't sleep or work. I steal into the hall to speak on the phone, not that it rings much. Just as the jackhammering starts, my mother becomes an invalid. My father has been dead for twenty-five years, and she's fared pretty well, but that's done. Her arteries are clogged with plaque like tubes with toothpaste, but she's brushed off the news and gone into cardiac arrest. A squat little machine that looks like Artoo-Detoo is attached to her by a vacuum cleaner hose, and my sister is holding a clipboard. Ellen is tapping it with a long, hard fingernail saying, "You have two choices, Ma, sign the form or dead. Which is it, Ma, the form or dead?" I am glancing from the machine to my mother, who looks like a chimp caught in a lab experiment. She trains her beady eyes on Ellen, as if she's being conned, but she takes the pen in her monkey paw and signs on for three more years of life—as well as a stroke and the twenty-four-hour care of home aides that Ellen and I will supervise. My mother and I don't like each other, don't see eye to eye, don't get along, but love is some-where in the room, and I feel responsible for her no matter what. It's like watching your own death.

As if Suzy has set in motion the butterfly effect, linking seemingly unrelated events, Richard invites me for a walk. After breakfast, he usually strides off by himself along the wooded paths that snake around the four small lakes dotting the gigantic rich people's estate where Yaddo is set. I feel happy, although I don't want to. The day I arrive, I see him in a little parlor off the dining room, a slender man with salt-and-pepper hair who looks autumnal in brown and gray gear except for the fancy, rectangular glasses he wears with flashes of orange and sapphire. He has a musical British voice and eyes that smile, although more often they sit catlike and watchful behind his specs. Human beings have an on/off switch that declares: you, yes; you, no. We smell each other and mirror neurons fire. Over the years I have mothed toward a few beautiful thugs, but it's the smart boys, the tender boys I prefer. Richard is married. He doesn't say much about his wife, Suzanne,* but he is married, and I am cutting down on opportunities for disliking myself.

And yet we are similar, we find, as we talk at meals: not depressed but not all that alive. He says that at seventeen he married a girl from his village, believing the baby she was carrying was his, or simply feeling responsible—or wanting sex on a regular basis and to play at being adult. They weren't in love, and there were issues of trust, and when the boy, Trevor,* was three Richard pulled himself out and he and Trevor, now a man, do not speak. Richard is unguarded, and I see his sorrow, and the story attracts me because he has saved himself but not escaped the consequences. Trevor is owed an apology, Richard feels, although he hasn't offered it. "Isn't there still time?" I ask, and he throws me a grumpy smile.

The day before my birthday, my friend Natalie and her daughter Maya drive to Yaddo from Massachusetts. Natalie and I have been pals since Barnard. Maya is twenty, at college, an artist who knows her worth—a gorgeous vegan spawn of the women's movement. When I knew Adele, I didn't ask her why, after Norman stabbed her, she stayed with him for two more years. She didn't press charges; he walked away with a suspended sentence for third-degree assault and spent fifteen days in a psychiatric ward. They had two young daughters who Norman visited on Sundays. I used to watch him in the elevator and imagine his writer's life. Famously, he debated Germaine Greer in Town Hall, decrying birth control and abortion. He didn't believe in equal rights for women, didn't see women as fully human, and yet his views were never dismantled by another man. How did he think his ideas went into his daughters?

*pseudonym

Natalie is one of the cool, slouchy girls who magnetized Kate and later kicked aside her motorcycle, went to law school, and had a kid. In the early '70s, when *Sexual Politics* made Kate a star and she was outed as a lesbian, Natalie and Fumio had an affair and went to Sweden. We drive to a restaurant and drink margaritas. She gives me a gift of a framed photograph of Kate and Fumio back in the day. They're on a bed, Fumio in the back, cross-legged and taking up no space. "Little bird," Kate calls him with a mouth in the shape of a shark. He could be a child, but if you look at his unsmiling face with its curtain of dark hair over his forehead, you see he isn't young and that he is a storage unit. During World War II, the boy with strong, brown legs was conscripted into the military, and his job was clearing out bodies at Hiroshima.

Kate is in the foreground, leaning on an elbow, wearing a long shirt and slacks. She takes up space, and her eyes are sad because she doesn't want to be married to her little bird, even though he makes their cage beautiful. She is already famous in a way that Warhol—who survives Valerie's attack—calls a commodity. But Kate and Fumio are our older artist friends, and they are luminous, the improbable mating of the boy marked by history and the fleshy odalisque made afraid of her amplitude by the writers she loves: D. H. Lawrence, Henry Miller, Mailer, even Genet. Fumio draws cartoons of his girl sprawled on a bed, her naked legs in the air, and he's off to the side, wielding his penis like Cupid's arrow about to pierce its mark. One summer, Bruce and I crash at a house on Fire Island, and Kate and Fumio visit. He rolls up his pants, dons a straw hat, and in the bay finds hundreds of clams with his toes that we transform into dinner for twelve.

Richard and I walk into the cool morning air, and we're alone on the paths strewn with wet leaves and fallen branches. He says his dad would disapprove of the untidiness. His father plays inside him, a compass pointing home—a man who wanted an education but was forced to become a tailor, like his father. We circle the lakes and our jackets swish, nearly touching. I am used to being alone and I like solitude, but existence without intimacy is flat and dull. Richard is describing his early days in New York when he'd go to a diner on Columbus Avenue and order eggs over easy and every day get porridge or waffles because no one could understand his accent. He'd eat the meal anyway, and I can see him, too polite to send it back, and I like his forbearance and idiocy. "It's my birthday," I blurt out, but don't say which one, although I think he can tell because a tear plops out. If you think there is a part of you that makes you unlovable, you will protect it like your child and show it to everyone. We walk and walk until we arrive at rose beds set out like the gardens of a French palace. The stalks are pruned, although a few bold blossoms persist.

We've arranged to meet in my studio a few days before, so he can read aloud his work. He arrives after dinner and sets his computer on a table in front of the couch. A fire is going, and there are flowers in a vase. I take a cushion on the floor. His hair glistens in the flickering light as he evokes himself at twenty-one, working in a no-hope clerk job in Birmingham after leaving Marylyn. He's not making enough to house and feed himself, and he feels stuck, and then he wanders into a museum and is stabbed with emotion by a John Millais painting. The picture's vibrant colors and message of hope, set against the backdrop of the soot-blackened city, wake him up. He's already met Meg,* the next woman he will be with, and she's at university, and he begins to study and in time is

*pseudonym

accepted, too. The piece is part of a book he's writing about how meaning is constructed in museum galleries and how space is interpreted wherever there are signs, and he reads two more sly essays, one about wildlife trails, the other about human exhibits, including slave auctions and the Paris morgue. I am moved by how he's invented himself. I say the writing is surprising and so vivid I can enter his world. He laughs, his mouth widening, his lips moving back from his teeth, and as light shoots from his eyes, I think: This is enough.

At the artist colony we're fourteen in all, quite the little microcosm of ages and personalities, and we take to playing a parlor game called Mafia, in which someone, randomly, draws a card that appoints him a hit man. I am routinely the first to be suspected and killed off. When I ask why, people say: "You look guilty." Richard, on the other hand, is trusted: no stray need escaping his cap. At the end of his stay, we drive to the airport and can't find the entrance, and he says it's a sign he shouldn't leave.

Have you ever longed to be a koala bear? It's not really that strange an appetite. What I'm getting at is choice—the amount we humans have to juggle. Have you ever wished to spend your life in an airport, presenting your shampoo vials to the security personnel, tenderly unwrapping your laptop from its case, arriving at your departure gate, only to learn that your flight has been delayed? You float in your bardo, off the ground by several inches, rocking gently on a glassy lake.

At dinner time, a koala bear has only one concern: Is this a eucalyptus leaf or isn't it? We, on the other hand, can eat anything and it makes us who we are. We need a larger frontal cortex, where memory and reasoning reside. We have to remember not to ingest the mushroom that killed Uncle Henry last week. We have to recall we had an Uncle Henry and understand the concept of last week. We are the only animals who can imagine *later*, who can fill in the blanks, who can see the nothing that is there, who can see ourselves as vanished as a magician's rabbit. And we can change partners.

When Richard and I say good-bye, we make no plans, but he returns home in order to leave again, a decision that isn't fair or kind but feels, he says, like coming back to life. When he left for Yaddo, he thought Suzanne was sick to death of him. "Roommates" is how he described them, and so her grief shocks them both. In time, when he extends his hand, I take it. He works in Arizona, and I move there, not realizing how much I will miss New York. It is nothing in comparison with the dislocation he feels.

When I write this piece, Natalie will say it is bracketed by men. "That's how you still define yourself." I concede she's right. Bruce used to go to NOW meetings with me. He was out picketing the *New York Times* for listing separate male and female want ads, a practice our protests ended. "How come you're always with a man?" I was asked in the early days of the movement, when women were carving out a separate space. Natalie will say, "Maya's generation, the girls don't operate the way we did." There was a time when being with a man advertised the capacity to attract one. If I'm honest, I will say it still does, although I was about to write the pleasure has washed out of me.

When Richard recalls Yaddo, he says our path was smoothed after dinner one night when I clear plates and silverware from the table—deftly, from the right, as I've been trained to do as a cater-waiter. He sees an act of service in my gesture, something soft and generous that hasn't surfaced before, and maybe he glimpses a French maid in my dipping at the waist. For me it's the morning I awake with an idea: consciousness and religion arrived together, the one mistaken for the other. I picture a gracile primate wandering across a savannah. Hearing hooves approach, she looks for escape in a tree and, finding none, registers the understanding in her head. She *hears* a thought, and it must feel like a voice originating from another source, a power greater than the animal and outside it. I want to share this notion, and the next thing I know *Richard* is in my head. We cross paths in the little parlor lined with books. There are throw pillows on the sofa and chairs, although they are straight-backed and uncomfortable. At first his hands rest on his thighs, and then he picks up a black stone with white stripes that someone has brought back from a hike. It's smooth as skin, and he rubs it absently. "Can you picture our ancestor?" I ask, and he says, "Picture her, I'm invaded by consciousness every day," and he talks about the numinous—moments that are terrifying and fascinating at the same time—like our awareness of death. I'm lost in this talk of thinking and dying, although I try not to show how much.

Where we live in Arizona, the coyotes have drunken parties at night, celebrating a kill—someone's small dog or a cat they've captured. Their joy is infectious. The animals are yellow with burning eyes and extra spring in their steps. In some traditions, the coyote is a wolf howling to feel air cross its throat. In others, the coyote is a lazy schemer whose plans don't work out.

At the start of a hike, I stand on the road while Richard studies trail maps. He explains where we are going, but I don't care. I know the trek will be arduous and hot and that I will not exactly enjoy it, rather want to go along and hope to see lizards and birds. Shade is beautiful in the desert, cutting a knife edge against glaring light, bleeding across wide, vacant space. One day, we arrive at the top of a hill, and Richard sees a higher point crowned by black, jutting rocks. As we scurry up, we realize we've come to the old wall of a fortified area. A small sign indicates an archaeological site, but it isn't marked to attract visitors. Everywhere are petroglyphs: designs scraped out on black desert varnish by people who lived in the region nine hundred years ago. I copy a stick design into my notebook that looks like a Giacometti figure—a pared-down, twig thing—a remnant of ourselves we carry inside.

Inside Richard, the remnant of memory is Suzanne. These days they are talking about what couldn't be said before. "How could you let him leave his wife?" asks a woman I slightly know, as we ride together on a train. She doesn't sound judgmental, more like a naturalist wondering where a scorpion stores its poison and how it feels to flex its pincers. "Richard decided," I say, but she knows I didn't put a gun to his head, and I know I didn't say, "Stop," fearing he might listen to me. Sometimes we feel we've stepped onto an escalator that doesn't deposit us anywhere, just keeps rising and falling, although we don't try to step off. The way we did it, leaping toward each other without a plan, is looking like a tendency: something leaning in your direction, a cat against your leg. Tendency is something that's almost irresistible but gives you an edge to play with, and it's the edge that gets you every time. Tendency is desire in the form of a question.

When, at sixty-two, I call Bruce, it's to ask for his copy of our divorce decree. I've lost mine, and I'm claiming Social Security early. In 1975, a few days before his second marriage, he divorced me in Haiti. He's unsmiling as he mounts the stairs of the brownstone where I live, and he doesn't make eye contact as he hands me the document. I watch him descend, feeling that something nasty is happening to us, even though we have cheated on each other and he is with Deborah and I am with Robert, whom I love.

He answers the phone in a soft voice. No time has passed. His daughter is thirty-one, his son twenty-six—the only people he knows who are related to him by blood. He's reading a book about Gandhi. Do I know which Western writer influenced Gandhi the most? Thoreau, I guess, and he says, "Tolstoy," and that makes sense, given his socialist conversion, and I remember the name of Tolstoy's estate, Yasnaya Polyana, because long ago Bruce taught it to me. When we get what we want, we often feel cheated of our yearning and turn against the prize. I don't want to do that anymore. I say, "Funny thing, all these years I am thinking I'm Laurie Stone, but the government claims it's an alias and that I'm really Mrs. Zimmer." And I am, all these years, fighting her, still her.

I am striding through the city to enter the common air. The wind cuts my cheeks and messes my hair. My mother dreams of her legs running for a bus. "I'm not young anymore," she says to the tall man with a mustache who guides her up the steps. "I wish I had your youth, darling, I wish you good health, you are so kind." I am walking on streets I can't get to, a blur of color and action. Richard is beside me, although we awake to a sky that looks like the cloudless blue eye of a noir killer.

I'm best in a foreign country where I don't understand the language and customs, and so everything is enigmatic and in my ignorance I attach a benign interpretation, or no meaning at all. I have the sensation of hanging by a silk thread and feeling air move across my skin. I'm not afraid of falling, because nothing is stronger than spider silk. If you wake me suddenly and ask, What is the thing you are proudest of? I will say: The women's movement and the way it changed the world.

LAURIE STONE is the author of *Starting with Serge, Close to the Bone,* and *Laughing in the Dark.* She has written for the

Village Voice, Ms., and *New York Woman*, was a theater critic for the *Nation*, and a critic-at-large on *Fresh Air*. She has received several grants, including the New York Foundation for the Arts, and was awarded the Nona Balakian prize in excellence in criticism from the National Book Critics Circle. Her essays have appeared in *TriQuarterly, Threepenny Review, Speakeasy*, and *Creative Nonfiction*. She is currently at work on *My Life as an Animal, a Memoir in Stories* and *Unmarked Trail: A Romance in Stories and a Guide to Setting Up a Writing Partnership*, with Richard Toon.

CHRIS HARDY

PAGING EMMA PEEL

Jane Ganahl

The year was 1968 and the world was exploding around me.

Bullets killed Martin and Bobby, antiwar protests at my high school nearly got me expelled, the judge's gavel at David Harris's trial (where I sat in the audience) pounded out the warning to all other draft resisters that jail would be the result of nonregistration, the Tet Offensive in Vietnam had left almost 60,000 dead on all sides. And my adolescent hormones were detonating like a nuclear blast.

All. Day. Long.

Jim Morrison wasn't just attractive, he was *soooo bitchin*! As was Paul McCartney, Peter Tork, and, of course, Mick Jagger. With just the opening bass notes of "Jumpin' Jack Flash," I felt a stirring south of my oversized belt buckle, and I wanted—I *needed*—something to do with my shaking hips, my anxious hands. But what, exactly? Although daunted by a pronounced lack of experience, I was pretty sure my constant daydreams about grabbing Mick's tush had to do with S-E-X. But that was foreign territory to me: a sixteen-year-old virgin tomboy whose skinny frame was occasionally mistaken for one of her many boy-pals.

I had begun to regret my years-long campaign to just be "one of the guys." It had begun in fifth grade—a Tet Offensive of my own—when my girlfriends had started getting all weird on me. They were no longer interested in catching frogs in the creek; instead, they wanted to work on their dance steps, their hairstyles, and more feminine athletic pursuits like tennis. Okay, and they were getting boobs and I was not. They were no longer like me. But—thanks to the testosterone god—the boys still were.

My male-worship began with the two in my family. I used to say that I was my brother's brother. Two years separated us, but my tall younger sibling was sometimes asked if he was my twin. He was a champion creek-walker and tadpole capturer when we were little, and then later, my dad got us both go-karts in which we careened around our three acres at dangerous speeds, like Evel Knievel. I was pretty sure I had the coolest brother in the world—and the coolest Dad. "Captain Bob" was a Pan Am pilot who flew into some of the world's most exotic ports of call, looked like Robert Young, and sang like Perry Como.

It was probably no surprise to anyone—least of all my mother, who had offered to school me in domestic arts, only to be stingingly rejected—that I would take after the men in my family instead of the women. What they did and how they moved in the world was just so much more . . . *interesting*! Who cared about crocheting and cooking, when you could build tree forts and drive go-karts? Mom wisely didn't try to alter my bent, probably realizing that I'd eventually have ample cause to join the female species.

In the meantime, even as my girlfriends were trying on nail polish, I was scraping the dirt from under my own nails and being invited to fewer and fewer sleepovers. It didn't seem like a sacrifice at all. I loved boys. I mean, I *really* loved boys. At that age, it was not a hormone-fueled love but a grand, operatic appreciation of everything male. The leonine way they moved, their confidence in the classroom, even the way they sometimes pummeled each other during recess. Given my own pugilistic tendencies—I had on more than one occasion rained my fists down on a classmate who teased me for being skinny—I found their violence fascinating.

So I campaigned to be one of them. I asked to be included in games of touch football, softball, and would insinuate myself into their recess conversations. Some of them told me to piss off; others took me under their smallish wings and showed me how to play. I'm not sure they liked me, but they tolerated me. And I was in heaven, being close enough to feel their sweat when they threw their arms around me on the field of battle, on that rare occasion when I carried the football or made it to first base.

It didn't occur to me in fifth grade that I'd never get to *second* base in heavy petting if I continued my antifeminization campaign. How were the boys supposed to see me as a girl when I reached eighth grade and became eligible to attend the Wood-side Elementary School dances, if I was slapping playing field dust off my pants? Could they accept me in a dress? Luckily, I always had at least one suitor who would escort me, but it was never the high-testosterone popular boys—always the sweaty-handed smart boys who ran the movie projector in class.

By the time I was sixteen, in 1968, I'd moved from being a physical tomboy to an intellectual one. I put the go-kart up on blocks, got involved in the male-heavy anti-war movement, and starting hanging out with brilliant Jewish boys from my Honors English class. I had small crushes on all three, but most especially on Michael, who was so smart he was doing a student internship at NASA, and had the cutest shaggy-dark hair and mustache. I sought to make him think of me differently than the tomboy who made him laugh in class when I told the teacher I thought Hester Prynne should have told both Dimmesdale and Chillingworth to shove it and torn that tacky "A" off her dress.

But Michael never responded to my feeble attempts at flirting; I was one of the boys, after all. My self-esteem began to crumble. I still wanted to be a savvy smart aleck like my guys, but realized that I'd have to become more *girlie* to be popular—and I'd always equated being girlie with being weak.

Alone in my bedroom, I'd stare in the mirror and wait for a new image to emerge. I'd try on miniskirts and makeup and I still looked awkward, like someone trying desperately hard to be someone she wasn't. I even practiced giggling behind my hand like my friend Debby, who always had lots of boys around her. But I gave up in tears. The face in the mirror was lost in a haze of adolescent confusion.

I also realized that I had no idea what I wanted to do with the life that loomed just beyond the parentally mandated four years of college. I had a vague sense of how I wanted my future to look: it would have a nonconformist bent and I would put my own stamp on the world. I would not necessarily be famous, but front and center in the world. I had no idea what profession I would choose, but it had to be daring and bold. Archaeologist? Firefighter? Political activist?

Every potential profession I imagined for myself was male-dominated, and I secretly reveled in the idea that my future would provide a cornucopia of testosterone. There would be men—many men—to date, to have sex with, to join in the struggle for human rights, to be inspired by. And I'd inspire them back. I wanted to be alone among the fraternity. I wanted to be queen bee and didn't really see the point of having too many girlfriends.

Would I get married? I wondered. Sure, why not? Everyone gets married these days. And look at the great power couples of history—they could not have done half of what they did without that other half. Louise Bryant had John Reed, right? Jane Fonda had Tom Hayden? Joan Baez had David Harris? And my mom had my dad, lucky lady. Besides, single women were such sad creatures! Everyone knew that. All you had to do was look at Margaret Wilson,* our church's choir director, a sixtyish spinster with hard features like Joan Crawford, a lonely woman who taught piano lessons and was the object of some pity around the church.

Jesus, I didn't want to end up like Margaret! So I surmised that marriage was both inevitable and necessary.

But I did not see myself as a parent. I always loathed babysitting and took no interest in my much younger cousins. I dismissed the idea of procreation, figuring mewling babies would be an impediment to both fun and my future as a swashbuckling . . . something. But what? Where did I fit in? What was I good at?

That all changed quickly, and most unexpectedly, in the fall of my junior year. On a Saturday night, I was invited to join my Jewish boys at one of their homes to see an episode of *The*

---

*pseudonym

Avengers—a British show I had heard about for two years but had never seen, since my parents believed TV was a sapper of creativity and intelligence and so they limited our couch time. The boys were big fans—of the show's winking satire on James Bond films, of the outlandish plots, but most especially of its female lead, Emma Peel, over whom they drooled frequently and annoyingly.

Perhaps it was the pot we smoked first, but I found myself practically trembling with excitement. Emma Peel—what a woman! She was thin and athletic as I was, smart as a whip, kicked ass on bad guys, wielded a mean fencing foil, fought for truth and justice—and looked incredibly hot in a leather cat suit and lavender lipstick. She was a tomboy—way more macho than John Steed—who still managed to bring men to their knees, and not just because she was karate-chopping them into submission.

She drove a Lotus like I did my go-kart, could interrogate a man by squeezing his head between her ankles, wore the coolest clothes I'd ever seen in my life, and was married—although that didn't seem to interfere with her quest to save the world from bad guys and flirt up a storm with Steed.

It was a revelation: A woman can be both a righteous fighter and a sexy babe at the same time! She can make her way in a man's world demanding respect, but also commanding lust. That, I thought, was what I wanted.

I went home, eager to test my new prototype. When I put the miniskirt back on and looked in the mirror, my body looked the same, but there was something different: my new-found role model gave me a dose of self-confidence I'd been lacking. Or maybe it was the new tube of Maybelline lavender lipstick? Either way, I felt ready to take on the world.

I tacked up a poster of Emma in my locker and galloped through my final years of high school and college with a mantra in my mind: What would Emma do?

A lot. I started auditioning for larger roles in plays, asked shy Michael on a date (which led to my smitten scientist naming a new compound, Janeite, after me), invited Joan Baez to speak on campus during the moratoriums, and was called to the principal's office for a serious scolding. *Fuck off!* I thought. *I'm fighting for truth and justice. Do not stand in Emma's path!*

In college, I continued my quixotic campaigns, fighting the Greek system in an Oregon college that was almost entirely populated by fraternities and sororities, staging anti-war protests, and generally raising hell. When Senator Hatfield came to dinner at our dorm, rather than dressing up as we were told, I rode my skateboard, drunk, into the dining room by way of protesting his close ties to Nixon. And during my junior year in Spain, I joined the student underground fighting Franco's policies—and shoved a guy up against the wall because he was harassing a friend in a disco. Emma did not cotton to this kind of sexist behavior.

I had to summon her when I fought with my parents to choose an English major over something that would actually make me money, saying that if I could not make a living with my heart, I would drop out and learn to weave baskets.

Emma was with me for years—but she disappeared when I fell in love. For temporary romance, I tended to pick men who were not as strong as I; for love, I picked men who dominated me completely. So feisty in dating mode, in love I would let my lover dictate my feelings, my direction, even my looks. For decades—starting with my first marriage at twenty-two—I rode a cruel see-saw between emulating Emma and, at the other end of the scale, a doormat.

I married my first husband—a gorgeous jock with long platinum hair—just out of college and watched my sense of self slip away. My housekeeping, my cooking, my looks, it appeared, did not live up to his standards—the usual stuff. But rather than telling him to fuck off, I took it personally and let it send my self-esteem over the side of the cliff. His coaching job dragged us to Southern California, then Texas, then Seattle, all in the first five years of marriage. His jock friends were around constantly, and I became a beer dispenser who would stay sober enough to make runs to the Circle K. Otherwise, I was completely, totally ignored.

For the first time in my life, I hated being the only female in the room. If I'd had Emma's foil, I'd have run them all through.

Perhaps determined to clip my sizeable wings once and for all, my husband started exhorting me almost immediately to have a baby. I wasn't excited about the prospect, but was so miserable that I thought perhaps if it made him happy, I would also be happy.

Two weeks shy of my twenty-sixth birthday, and after a dangerously long and arduous labor, Erin was born. I felt the superhero in me return when I looked down at her perfect face and was suddenly filled with the courage of a lioness. *Baby,* I thought, *it's probably going to be just you and me. But we can do this.*

Soon after, we were back home in California, where I've raised her on my own ever since. Single parenting was a struggle, but Erin turned out to be a source of strength—the rudder of my sometimes storm-tossed ship. As she grew, she never feared for her own strength as I did, nor stressed about her femaleness. I mean, this girl was wearing tutus when she was barely old enough to walk and never had the slightest inclination to leave her easels for the soccer field. Other than that, I was pretty sure she was my DNA.

I returned to the habit of summoning Emma when I plunged into newspaper writing. I covered the men's clubs of City Hall politics, rock music criticism—even the occasional sports story. At San Francisco City Hall, I regularly got anonymous voice mail messages suggesting I only got my story tips by "fucking around." I somehow doubt Woodward and Bernstein ever got such messages, and I somehow considered them a badge of courage.

Besides, I *was* fucking around. Just not for work reasons. It became clear—especially after my second marriage crashed and burned for the same reasons as the first—that I was much better off in casual relationships. So I had many. I figured it would only be a matter of time before I married again.

But it didn't happen.

As I pushed past forty-five and approached fifty, I began to feel invisible. Men who used to make beelines for me at parties started looking distractedly over my head, perhaps searching for a younger version of me in the crowd. I felt crushed and angry, helpless to turn back the tide.

But this sea change also provided a sterling silver lining. After I summoned Emma yet again and decided to make the best of things as a long-term single, independent woman, I found my stride—and my true calling. I began to write a Sunday column for the tenth-largest paper in the country about single life—the great parts about it, the not-so-great, the awful dates, the sheepish desire to be paired. It was a huge hit, and sometimes controversial. I was roundly excoriated for being a "femi-Nazi"—up to and including a denouncement by Rush Limbaugh on the air. (Alas that I could not conjure Emma to poke the fat bastard with her foil; I had to suffice with a smug smile to myself that I had finally arrived.)

The column led to editing a women's anthology, and after that, my own memoir, which was bought for a TV series. I became a mouthpiece for single living and even appeared on the *Today Show*. My grief at losing the eye of men was replaced by my joy in finding the ears of women; I was deluged weekly for five years with e-mails and letters thanking me for my bold opinions and saying how my columns had helped them in their quest to find equilibrium in an unmarried world.

My middle age has been a remarkable time—and a stunning reversal of where I thought I'd end up. When I was young, I thought I would treasure married life, being among men friends, and child free. In fact, my women friends, my single life, and my daughter have afforded me far greater joy than men ever did.

I almost feel like writing a thank-you note to the male species for turning away from me. It was only when I started to lose my hold on men that they lost their hold on me, and I was able to accomplish what I might have years ago, if not for my bad decision making and utter enthrallment with testosterone. I had to stop believing in the mirror of their faces and believe in the strengths I saw reflected in my increasingly lined eyes.

It's not that I hate men now—I still adore them. I've just stopped handing over my self-esteem to them. I'd like to think that this now makes me an ideal candidate for a fabulous relationship, one based on mutual respect and shared strengths. And that may happen . . . and it might not. The beauty is that nowadays I'm free to want men for all the same reasons I wanted them in fifth grade. But now, if they don't want me back, I know I'll be just fine.

Where did Emma go? She's still around, of course, in my heart and in my DVD collection—though I think I've learned from her pretty much all I can.

Now I see her spirit being re-channeled into the next generation.

"Mom, the developers are taking their bulldozers into my client's property, despite our restraining order," said my daughter, the newly minted environmental lawyer, on the phone recently. "I might have to physically get in front of them to get them to stop."

I told her I wasn't worried—I knew she could kick their butts. "Just be sure," I told her, "to wear your lavender lipstick."

JANE GANAHL has been a journalist, editor, author, consultant, and community organizer in San Francisco for twenty-five years. She is the author of the novelized memoir *Naked on the Page: The Misadventures of My Unmarried Midlife* (Viking), which is in development for a TV series. She is also the editor of the anthology *Single Woman of a Certain Age* (2009 New World Library paperback) and has contributed essays to several anthologies. Ganahl wrote the column "Single Minded" for the *San Francisco Chronicle*. She contributes regularly to the *Huffington Post*. Her work has appeared online—salon.com, rollingstone.com, etc.—and in such magazines as *Harper's Bazaar*. Ganahl is cofounder and artistic director of Litquake, San Francisco's annual literary festival, which, in 2008, drew more than 450 writers and more than 10,000 attendees. Her Web site is http://www.jane ganahl.com.

TERRY LORANT

SAYING GOOD-BYE

Michael Bader

What the hell am I doing here? Sitting in a hospital room in Kansas City, watching my father as he pretends to understand something a visitor is saying, pretending because I know that the cancer in his brain makes him confused most of the time. It isn't that I question my decision to come and visit him; it's that I know it's for the last time. I'm leaving in a few minutes to return to San Francisco.

I imagine standing up, crossing over to his bedside, and saying, "I'm leaving now, Dad,

243

and . . ." And what? Not "see you later" or "take care of yourself" as I usually do with him, as I suppose I usually do with everyone I leave, whether it's my wife when I leave for work in the morning, or a casual friend after a chance meeting in the supermarket. "See you later . . . take care." No. But am I supposed to say something honest like "I've always loved you, Dad, except when I imagined smashing your face with a baseball bat because I thought you ruined my life," or just something small and comforting like "I have to go, Dad . . . I'll be thinking about you, love ya"?

I mean, is this supposed to be an *important moment*, like the farewell scene in *Star Trek 2*, where a dying Spock touches Kirk's hand through the glass and says, "Live long and prosper"? For a minute, I feel detached from my body, floating up into space, looking down on the room, on my father, his diminished physique, bald head, and a face inscribed in my memories and dreams, and me sitting across from him. But me at six or twelve or eighteen. Certainly not fifty-five. Fifty-five? What happened? Are you fucking kidding me? And now, this fifty-five-year-old man is going to get up and say good-bye forever to his father?

Impossible. Despite the fact that this is supposed to be what happens—parents die—to me, it seems insane. How could this possibly be the natural order of things? I've never been in a more *un*-natural situation in my life. Other folks might think my father is in his eighties; I know he's really in his forties and I'm a kid. When I was young, very young, my father was the master of the universe. He'd go off to work in Manhattan on the train every day. He looked like Don Draper on *Mad Men*. Here's how great my father was: I once witnessed our family doctor, Dr. Lamberto, give him a penicillin injection in his left bicep. My father didn't flinch. Not even a little. In those days, the prospect of a shot was utterly terrifying to me. But my father was so strong that he felt neither fear nor pain. Here's another example of his greatness: When we were down at the Jersey Shore in the summer, my father would put me on his shoulders and go out into the ocean and stand while waves either carried us up and down or crashed over us. A wave might get him, but he'd make sure it didn't get me.

My father wasn't just great in those days, he was a great *man*. He was the ultimate of masculinity. And his masculine power wasn't just physical but mental. For example, he knew everything. He worked for Bell Telephone Laboratories and probably designed Telstar, the video phone, microwave technology, and the first computer. I once found blue books from exams he took in undergraduate mathematics classes at Yale and would copy them over, imagining that the equations were the key to space travel or nuclear fission. I remember once, in fifth grade, when being a loudmouth got me in trouble and my father's incalculable brilliance saved the day. I was complaining in class about the uselessness of studying history. The teacher, fed up, told me that if I thought I was so smart, well, then I'd just have to justify my view in a formal debate on the subject the next day. Resolved: There is no value whatsoever in studying history. I went home, distraught and embarrassed, and asked my father for help. He thought for a moment and then said, "Well, Michael, you could always just say this: There are three great problems currently facing mankind—Overpopulation, Nuclear Disarmament, and Civil Rights. Now, since these are all new problems, how can History possibly help us?" He said it with authority. Of course! A devastating and irrefutable argument! Suddenly, all seemed right with the world. My father was right again. I simply repeated his words the next day in the debate. I have some vague memory that the teacher and the opposition were stunned by my argument. I probably forgot how, after repeating the words of the Oracle, I realized I had nothing else to say because I didn't really know what I was talking about.

I could pretend to be my father, but eventually the pretense wore off. God knows I tried. I was desperate for his love, and if I couldn't get it directly I wanted to get it indirectly, to at least be like him. I wanted to be around his maleness, to bask in it, plug in to it, somehow. In the mornings, my father had a long bathroom ritual. I'd sometimes go into his bathroom to tell him something and be hit with a mélange of olfactory sensations that I can remember to this day. Today, those smells would no doubt trigger projectile vomiting, but in those days they equaled maleness because they were associated with my father: Mennen, Old Spice, Barbasol, Vitalis, Kent cigarettes, and the human GI tract, and all were perfused by the steamy warmth of his recent hot shower. I loved it.

Here's the thing, though, about identification: sometimes, it's a poor substitute for the real thing. Sometimes, it's the only way of maintaining a connection with a parent who can't have a real relationship with you. It's sort of the best that you, as a kid, can do. We want and need to be connected to a parent. We can't live without it, actually. But if that connection is missing, then we substitute the next best thing—trying to be *like* that parent. However, when the normal process of identification becomes overburdened with this additional meaning, it gets screwed up. The parent isn't taking you under his or her wing, isn't actually interested in your development, isn't present in a way that lets you see what it's *really* like to be a man or a woman. You have to guess, infer it from outward behavior, or imagine it in your fantasy life, and the outcome is often something artificial, confused, or unrealistic.

Like being the master of the universe. Like never feeling pain or fear. Like being able to solve any problem and protect anyone or anything that needs protecting. Like always being so smart and knowledgeable about everything that you're never ever wrong. I suppose I thought that this was what being a man was all about.

It's not. Competence and strength don't come out of one's mind and body fully formed. For example, when I took up golf, I went through a period where I actually believed that there was something innately wrong with my body, something that prevented me from hitting the ball a long way, even though all the evidence contradicted this. My real problem was that I couldn't let myself learn, couldn't let myself be bad at something with the optimistic faith that I could improve. A golf instructor once told me that many amateur golfers were three consecutive bad shots away from total madness. I was supposed to just do it well from the start. I was supposed to know. If someone stumped me in an argument, I'd feel shame. If I was afraid of a conflict, I'd feel like a coward. If I avoided dangers, I was weak. I kept failing in my attempts to do the impossible and that was simply unforgivable. I later learned, shortly before his death, that my father had to give up golf because it was too frustrating. He railed against helplessness and imperfection. It took me a lifetime to learn that real men accept both. Sometimes, even Tiger Woods hits a bad shot.

Of course, as I grew up, my father couldn't possibly survive the rarified atmosphere of such an impossibly high pedestal. I find myself wishing he could have enjoyed it more while he was up there. I liked having a father I looked up to. He should have let himself take pleasure in that. After all, the passage of time and a kid's growing awareness of reality eventually temper these idealizations all on their own. Unfortunately, my father couldn't enjoy being my hero, couldn't feel blessed by the opportunities I gave him to show me how wonderful it was to be a man; couldn't enjoy turning our relationship into a mutual admiration society. I think he felt guilty about it, or thought that such pleasure wasn't very masculine. Instead, he competed with me, bullied me. We argued a lot at the dinner table and he always won. He drank too much and had a temper, which he'd periodically lose, reducing me to a quivering jellyfish. And he never, with one exception, conveyed any pleasure or pride in having me for a son. In ninth grade, I played the alto saxophone in the high school symphony orchestra, and that spring, the spring of 1967, the greatest classical alto saxophonist in the world—Siguard Rascher— came to play a concert with us. I got to play a simple duet with Rascher. My mother told me that, during this duet, my father grabbed her arm and whispered to her how beautiful we sounded! One compliment, one time, told only to my mother and not me—and yet it brings tears to my eyes as I remember it. The tears come from the contrast between the memory and everyday life—it's like realizing how cold you are only when you enter a warm house.

My father couldn't help me figure out how to be a man because, it seemed to me, he didn't want me to be one.

As I write this, I'm aware of some guilt and embarrassment. Ahh—okay, the internal chorus is warming up: "Stop being such a goddamn victim, Bader! Grow up already! Get over it!" I'd have more sympathy for these voices, were it not for the fact that they were there even when I was young, presumably young enough to be entitled to a complaint or two. But I *always* thought that feeling sorry for myself was pathetic. My mother was a victim. Women were victims. Weaklings, not men, were victims. Besides, isn't blaming a parent for everything a sign that your relationship is still unresolved? In today's climate in particular, to resolve your childhood issues means to get to a place where you forgive your parents. No room for victims here.

I found myself thinking that my father's post-cancer bald

head made him look a little like Junior Soprano, Tony's uncle on *The Sopranos*. At the end of the first season, Tony Soprano is sitting in his therapist's office and the therapist confronts him with the likelihood that his mother, Livia, has conspired with Uncle Junior to have Tony killed. Suddenly, Tony leaps up, knocks over a table, grabs the therapist by the throat, and yells: "*That's my mother we're talking about. Not some screw-up in Attica, stabbing you in the shower. See, we're through, you and I. We're finished. You're lucky if I don't break your face in fifty thousand pieces.*"

No way Tony Soprano was a whiner, a victim of a bad parenting. He'd rather do anything, even assault his therapist, than have to listen to that crap. Of course, another word for "that crap" was *truth*. And I suppose that all of us would rather be, as the psychoanalyst W. R. D. Fairbairn once put it, "sinners in heaven than saints in hell." It's easier to consider that our parents were ultimately benign and that our suffering was our own fault.

Looking back, I can see the Tony Soprano inside me—no, not because I always wanted to own a strip club like the Bada Bing—but because, like Tony, I kept giving my parents chances to redeem themselves. As I got older, I'd ask my father to help write a talk I had to give, question him about politics, or ask for advice about girls, not so much because I needed his wisdom but because I imagined that these roles would make us both happy. They didn't. In each case, he'd take over like he did with the Great Fifth-Grade History Debate. He'd usually lecture me or try to say something profound. He felt he needed to be William Jennings Bryan, when all I wanted was a real-life Dad. And if he couldn't be great, he felt he had nothing to offer. That was both his cross to bear and mine. I finally confronted him about it when he had failed to respond to the seventh article I'd had published in a professional journal. Chagrined, he admitted that he worried that if he didn't have a brilliant response or critique, I'd be disappointed. I told him that "Looks great, son . . . congratulations!" would more than suffice. He said that he understood, but he continued till the end to follow the twisted edict "If you don't have something brilliant to say, then don't say anything at all."

Still, my father couldn't shake his fear of disappointing me. A few years before he died, I wrote to friends and family about a very scary diagnosis that my wife, Margot, had recently received. Most friends and family wrote back and said the usual comforting things—"I'm so sorry . . . You must be upset . . . Let me know if you need anything." My father, however, wrote: "Life comes at you sometimes like a thief in the night. Your life seems to be in fine order, breaks are going your way and then as if from nowhere, dire news. . . . There is an old saying that goes 'God enters through the wound.' Our spiritual hunger is most acute when we are most vulnerable." A thief in the night, God, wounds, spiritual hunger—uh, well, okay, but what about Margot? I'm absolutely sure that if my father had had the energy in the hospital that day, he'd be talking to me about Ernest Becker's views in his book *The Denial of Death*. And frankly, God had better prepare him or herself for my father's lecture about the perils of organized religion!

He thought he was pleasing me, but, instead, he was making it hard for us to make real contact, contact that both of us hungered for so much. That absence haunted my life. I'll never forgive this man, but perhaps I can give up my private campaign against him. Giving up is sadder than forgiveness, but also liberating. It was the only way that I could possibly free myself from the tyranny of impossible expectations—of him and of myself.

As I sit there watching this sick and vulnerable father, his second wife, my stepmother, Dori, climbs into bed with him and rubs his head and sings "Send In the Clowns" to him. At first, he looks annoyed, but she ignores it. He relaxes, smiles, and tries to sing along—"Isn't it rich? Aren't we a pair? Me here at last on the ground, you in mid-air . . . send in the clowns." For a moment, he seems content. That's the key, of course, to getting through to my father. Just plunge ahead and smother him with love, whether or not he wants it. And above all, be immune to his crankiness. If he doesn't feel he has to please you or live up to your expectations, he can relax and be himself.

Dori's way of interacting with my father is so different than was my mother's. My mother would take his moods personally, feel rejected, and sulk, a process that would lead to frequent cold wars between them. These wars grew over time; given their histories, I suppose you could say that they came by them honestly. The seeds were planted quite early in their relationship. In the last years of their respective lives, both my parents told me a story about a conversation they'd had a week before they were married.

My mother had been working in a bank when she and my father first met. She loved her job. She loved the fact that it was social, that she could help people and get appreciation in return, and that she had some financial independence. The week before their wedding, my mother told my father that she was quitting her job because it was now his job to support her, and that her mother had told her that "married women didn't work." In her account of this conversation, my mother admitted that in fact she had liked working but felt that she was supposed to be a mother and housewife and be taken care of. It was a role that her mother and sisters had always aspired to, and she couldn't imagine making a different choice.

My father remembered accepting this pronouncement calmly and agreeably because that was also his sense of how women were supposed to be. He also remembered feeling a sharp sense of disappointment and resentment. He had liked the fact that my mother seemed so independent and buoyant, and, on a level that was barely conscious, felt the weight on his shoulders begin to grow. My siblings and I—with all of our expectations and needs—became three of those weights.

My visit is nearing its end. Dori leaves the room. It's snowing outside and cold, very cold there in Kansas City. I've been in California so long that I've come to consciously hate the cold. It brings back too many unpleasant memories of my childhood in New Jersey. This time, though, it brings back a nice one. November 9, 1958, was a Sunday and it was my birthday. My "present" was to be able to go with my father into New York City to visit the Museum of Natural History. It was a cold day, crispy cold. Because it was Sunday morning, there were no crowds. We bought hot roasted chestnuts from a street vendor. I was with my father, alone. Not watching him from a distance, not sharing him with anyone, heading toward a place that had special meaning only to me. The previous year, our family had gone to the Museum of Natural History and I was given a sample of different rocks, among them a beautiful piece of quartz crystal. I couldn't stop talking about it.

For some reason, the museum was closed on this Sunday. We returned home and he bought me a toy as a substitute, a toy that soon broke. I couldn't explain to him that the only thing that really mattered to me was that I got to be with him. Sadly, he couldn't see that either. In my own therapy, I've always emphasized the latter half of that memory, the one filled with disappointment and misunderstanding. But as I sit here in this hospital room, finally alone again with my father, I think of the first part, the part where we're together and the air is cold and the chestnuts are warm and all is right with the world.

We don't resolve relationships with parents as much as accept them. What's done is done. No one can make up for anything at a deathbed. If any restitution gets made, it has to come earlier. I made such an attempt in my own limited way several years earlier at my father's eightieth birthday celebration. My wife and I went back to Kansas City to celebrate the occasion. His birthday was always complicated for me because it's the same day as mine and, for most of my life, my father would "forget" to acknowledge it. Still, this was a big occasion, and I worked hard on a toast for him. I thought to myself, What could I say to my father that would mean the most to him, what words would be absolutely specific to him and our relationship? When the time came, I stood up and said, "My father is the smartest man I know and I'm blessed to have inherited some of that." But then I added this: "Even though he and I have been through a lot, a lot of conflict, a lot of pain, I never for one moment doubted that he loved me, that despite everything else, I always understood this one irreducible truth."

I knew that this was what my father most needed to hear from me, not that I loved him but that I knew he loved me. I think sometimes we focus on the importance of being loved and fail to appreciate the need to be recognized as *loving*. Maybe, in the end, that's what reconciliation is about. It's not about forgiveness as much as it's about recognizing our parents' common humanity, seeing that even as they hurt you, sometimes grievously, they were also capable of feeling love; that they were endowed, just like you, with the capacity for love.

My father wrote me several days later and, in his inimitable way, said, "Events under the heading of 'reconciliation' stand alone in my mind as the greatest act of grace I have been granted. To be forgiven and to be loved by those you have hurt so deeply in the past is miraculous. You never gave up on me and for that I shall be forever grateful. Thank you Michael, my son, my amazing son."

It's time to leave. I get up, walk over to his bed, and say,

"Dad, I have to go now." I lean over and kiss him. He looks at me, clear-sighted, and says, "Look, if I don't recover from this, I want you to know that I've always loved you and been proud of you."

"I've always loved you, too," I reply. "And I always wanted to be like you . . . and I am . . . in here," and point to my heart.

And then I left.

MICHAEL BADER is a clinical psychologist and psychoanalyst in private practice in San Francisco. He is the author of two books about sexuality: *Arousal: The Secret Logic of Sexuality* and *Male Sexuality: Why Women Don't Understand It—and Men Don't Either.* Michael has written extensively in both online and print magazines and journals about the interplay of psychology, popular culture, and politics. In addition to his writing and private practice, he helped found and currently teaches in a progressive leadership development and organizational change program called the Institute for Change, which is affiliated with the largest and fastest-growing labor union in the country, the Service Employees International Union. He has also written about golf, but, like his handicap, he doesn't usually broadcast that fact. His Web site is http://www.michaelbader.com.

TURNING SOIXANTE-DIX

Barbara Abercrombie

"Are you still writing, are you still teaching?" old friends ask. This question always takes me by surprise. Why wouldn't I be?

My dream, my fantasy as a child, was to become famous. I remember being six years old and imagining a camera following me around the backyard as I talked to my invisible interviewer. Like a miniature Martha Stewart, I discussed the flowers. *Oh, yes, I love flowers. These are marigolds. I planted the seeds myself.*

255

This was long before video cameras, *People* magazine, and the cult of celebrity. My family didn't even own a television set in those days so I'm not sure how I knew about fame, or what my grasp of it could possibly have been, but that moment of being in the imaginary spotlight, explaining myself and the garden, is a vivid memory. Maybe I connected being famous with being popular—and if I were popular I'd be loved. Or was it a matter of being heard? Having a voice?

All this might lead you to the conclusion that I had a deprived and lonely childhood—but no, I was born into a normal, suburban, middle-class family. My mother was a housewife and played classical piano, my father was in charge of the Woolworth lightbulb accounts for General Electric and commuted from Westchester County into New York City every day. (The constant admonishment of my childhood was "Better light, better sight!") When I was five, a baby brother arrived on the scene. Which possibly could be a clue to my sudden desire for fame.

My father took a lot of home movies of my baby brother during his first Christmas with us. There he is at six months, adorable in his red Santa jammies, cuddled and cooed over by my mother. And there's me, five years old, skinny, white-blond hair, socks drooping, dancing my heart out for the camera in front of the Christmas tree. Frantic for attention, wanting to be the star, looking totally unhinged and desperate. To watch this old home movie makes you want to reach out and pat the kid and say, Hey, it's all right. You're loved, too.

Around the time of my backyard interview about the marigolds, I wrote and illustrated my first book: *The Butterfly Who Flew Too Close to the Sun*. It was about eight pages long and the ending was fairly tragic—the butterfly melted. Since I was only six years old, I doubt this was a metaphor for fame and its consequences; I simply loved drama and excitement.

One day in first grade, during Show & Tell, I announced that I had an older brother and sister who were movie stars in Hollywood. This of course was a huge lie—but I had nothing interesting to show or to tell that day and I didn't want to bore anybody. My lie had an electrifying effect on the entire elementary school: I became popular overnight. Kids would gather around me and ask questions about my movie star brother and sister, and the more questions they asked, the more lies I had to tell. This all grew into what felt like a nightmare. When anyone asked what my fictitious siblings were filming, I had to make up whole movie plots. One day, when a friend was visiting my house and asked where they lived when they were home from Hollywood, in desperation I described an entire apartment hidden away up in the attic that we were not allowed to go up to see. In the midst of all this, my mother came to school and my teacher noted with surprise how young she looked to have grown children in Hollywood. My mother was quite startled and my lie was exposed. Later she said to me, "You have a wonderful imagination, but you must always tell the truth."

This experience had such a profound effect on me that I have not lied since I was in first grade. A few years ago I wrote a children's picture book based on the experience. The little boy in my book has lied to his class, telling them he has a pet lion at home. When the class wants to plan a field trip to his house to see his lion, he confesses to his mother the lie he's told, and she tells him exactly what my mother told me. But instead of sitting in the kitchen weeping with shame and embarrassment, which is what I did, the little boy writes and illustrates a book about his lion and explains to the class that it wasn't a lie exactly, it was real in his imagination.

I loved making up stories. My favorite game as a child was to draw people on paper, cut them out, and then create imaginary houses and towns for them to live in. Hour after hour, I'd sit on the living room floor and move them through the stories I made up about their lives. In fifth grade, when Mrs. Safro had us all stand in front of the class and tell what we wanted to be when we grew up, I said that I was going to write books.

In her class we had story hour every Friday afternoon—we'd all read something we'd written the previous week. I discovered that if I kept my story going, wrote it in chapters and left my heroine in dire straits every Friday afternoon to be continued (steep cliffs, typhoons, and runaway trains were involved), kids would flock around and ask me, What happens next? I was home free. I was popular, if not famous, and I was a storyteller, which gave me permission to tell the very best lies I could come up with.

At age eleven I wrote a play, cast it with kids in my neighborhood, gave myself the starring role, directed it and produced it in my backyard. Shortly after rehearsals began, one of my actors—he was my next-door neighbor, nine years old, a bit nerdy—knocked on my front door and said, "Nobody wants to be in your play. You're too bossy."

I was crushed. I hid in my house and cried. When I recovered, I gathered my cast together and made a little speech. I promised to be a less bossy star, director, producer, writer—maybe even give them all a few more lines. And the show did go on—all the parents came and sat on the hill in our backyard (I was also the ticket seller and usher). It was a huge success. And I loved acting. An audience! People laughing and clapping right there in front of you! It was even more fun than sitting around making up stories and moving my paper people through their lives.

I wasn't smart about many things as a teenager, but I was brilliant when I realized acting would be easier, and probably a lot more exciting, than writing.

My parents, even though they were avid theatergoers, were not thrilled with my choice of career. "You should get an English degree and then if something happens to your husband you'll be able to support yourself by teaching," said my father. I rolled my eyes at this idea and dropped out of college.

As I was packing my bags at age nineteen to move to New York to become an actress, my father said to me, "You're so stubborn and stupid you'll probably make it." It always shocks my friends when I tell them what he said, but he was right, and I understood that it was said with love and even admiration. I was indeed stubborn, and I was stupid in the sense that I ignored the fact that there were tens of thousands of other girls my age headed for New York and Hollywood with the same dream. The odds for making it were not terrific.

But "making it" can have many interpretations. In New York, after a sobering few months working in ladies handbags at Saks Fifth Avenue and selling subscriptions to the *New York Times* over the phone at night, I began to support myself by acting—on Broadway, cross-country tours, and on television. I had the strange distinction of playing ingénues in more failed Broadway plays than any other actress my age. But as far as I was concerned, earning a living doing something I loved, and had done for fun as a kid, was making it.

Along with writing, and then acting, I'd always dreamed of having a large family. I never doubted for a minute that I wanted to get married and have at least five children, and this never seemed incompatible with my feminist view of life.

One cold snowy day in February, I flew from New York down to Puerto Rico to sit in the sun for a few days; I was due back in New York the following week to do a try-out of a play at the Actors Studio. The day after I arrived, I went into the bar in the small hotel where I was staying and met my first husband. He was a lieutenant in the navy and on his way to Vietnam. We were married three weeks later in New York.

I followed him to Vietnam and we lived in Saigon for a year. After returning to the States, I got pregnant and we had our first child, a daughter, in January 1966. A second daughter followed in December. My husband left the navy and we moved to Los Angeles, where he became a stockbroker, and I went briefly back to acting. But in 1968 I had no role models for juggling a career and a family; I could not find a way to be both a good mother to two babies and also be a working actress. I did one television show, but my heart wasn't in it anymore. All I did was worry about the temporary babysitter I'd hired to look after my little girls.

I became a stay-at-home mom, scrubbing floors to hospital standards, knitting miles of afghans, tearing up a whole back-yard to grow vegetables, refinishing furniture, and making a lot of salt-dough ornaments and cookies over the holidays. And sometimes I wrote stories.

I got pregnant again. And for the first seven months all was the same as in my earlier pregnancies—no morning sick-ness, no problems. I always loved being pregnant—having a big belly, a baby moving inside me; I was my own universe, accomplishing something even if I just sat on the beach per-fectly still and gazed at the ocean. I read Shirley Jackson's *Life among the Savages*, based on her children and her life as a writer, and wanted to do the same—write books, yet have this lively family life with many children. I kept an on again/off again journal and occasionally worked on a mystery novel, but very little serious writing got done while I was pregnant.

Early in my eighth month, after a routine blood test, the doctor asked if we'd had any problems with RH factor in my other pregnancies. I was O negative and it turned out my husband was O positive, though his naval medical records, in a serious error, stated he was O negative too. So there was a problem. I had amniocentesis before anyone had ever heard of it. I went into the hospital for fetal blood transfusions. I believed everything was going to be fine.

I went into labor a few weeks later. When we got to the hospital and the doctor examined me, he told me he was giving me a special drug, like a super martini that would make me feel wonderful. "The olive will be a problem," I said. And then I got a shot that put me out like a light and when I woke up my husband was sitting on my bed, holding my hand. Our baby had been born dead. Born dead. How could those two opposing words make sense?

We dismantled the nursery. My husband couldn't cope with grief and believed the way to get through this was to ignore it, not to think or talk about it. A lot of people told me how lucky I was to have my two daughters. I knew this of course, but I grieved for my third daughter.

I realized very clearly in the months afterward that I had to put all my love and passion and energy into something new, that maybe if I just focused on writing once and for all I could get through this.

One day, feeling old at age thirty-two and very scared, I signed up to take a creative writing class in a local community college. Even though I'd been writing off and on for years, I'd never taken a writing class or been in a workshop. I figured if it was too terrifying, I'd just quit. As it turned out, I took the same class from the same wonderful teacher, a poet, for eight semesters. I wrote two novels that didn't get published and many poems that did. I got so excited about poetry that I volunteered in my girls' school and became known as the Poetry Lady. Once a week for a year I appeared in each class to read poems and have all the kids write poems of their own. I was my daughters' worst nightmare: The Poetry Lady was coming to their classroom and she was their mother.

Out of this year of volunteering came my first published book, an introduction to poetry for children. And then my first novel sold. I had discovered that writing and having a family worked for me—I believed I could do both 100 percent. And for a number of years this was true. I published more novels, a few more books for kids, as well as poems and essays. The very strange thing is that I also ended up fulfilling my father's advice about teaching, which I had ridiculed years before.

My marriage began to unravel. After a long, painful pulling apart, my husband and I officially separated twenty-six years after we met in Puerto Rico, and I needed a job. I was fifty years old, a college dropout and by then a writer who was deeply blocked and couldn't write. I had no English degree, but "something had happened to my husband" and I began to support myself by teaching writing workshops. (This was after my father died, but even today, when I'm walking around the UCLA campus where I teach in the Extension program, I'll have conversations with him in my head: *You were right, Papa—but look! I'm doing it without an English degree!*) Someone once said you teach the class you need to take. Teaching my students how to move beyond their fear and blocks, I, too, moved past my own and began to write again.

I was single for seven years before remarrying, and in those years found that the sudden loneliness of divorce, the single-ness, the sense of failure and loss, were devastating. And yet later I realized that I didn't grow up until I was divorced. Before divorce, I had assumed a smooth and easy personal life. At one point, I believed that I had cleverly and seamlessly combined my work with raising my children. And I had believed, in my protected married bubble, that I was independent. None of the above proved to be true.

On my next birthday I will turn *soixante-dix*. (Oh, it sounds so much better in French!) I remind myself that I'm Tina Turner's age.

I'm happier than I've ever been in my life, and I find this astonishing. A lot of happiness is luck, of course—good health, work that is loved, finding the right person to share your life with. But now I recognize and pay attention to luck, hang onto it and am grateful for it. The combined family I share with my second husband is the large family I've always wanted—with grandchildren and stepchildren. My baby brother became one of my best friends. When he visits, we share a bottle of wine and argue about who was loved more. He claims I was, I say he was. He brings up the movie of me dancing in front of the Christmas tree and we laugh.

But there are days when I realize that the years are marching faster and faster toward a finite point in the future. I had breast cancer just before my second wedding, and two years ago my husband had a quadruple heart bypass, and last year a mild stroke. The chance of losing one another, a pretty sure bet as these happy years spin by, puts everything in perspective. *This is it.*

For a writer, at least this one, there's no culmination, no moment of thinking you've arrived, finished your work, pulled it off, and are done. It's like there are ledges you get to rest on as you climb up the face of a mountain. The first poem or essay published, the first book. When you publish a novel, you think the world will stop dead in its tracks, but it doesn't. There's always another book to write and to get published, the book that will be so much better—deeper and truer than the last one. You do this work uncertain most of the time and wondering if you'll ever publish again. It's a high-wire act right up the face of the mountain.

On good days, when I look in the mirror, I see a woman who didn't become famous, whose writing output and success has been modest in the extreme, but who loves books and stories and teaching, who is still playing with her paper people, moving them through imaginary lives, and still trying to guide her students past their fears and toward their own writing careers. A woman lucky enough to make a living doing what she did for fun as a kid.

So, yes, I'm still writing, still teaching, I'll always be writing, and I hope to still be teaching when I'm *quatre-vingt-dix*.

BARBARA ABERCROMBIE teaches at UCLA Extension and conducts writing workshops for the Wellness Community. She has published novels, children's books, essays, poetry, and articles. Her latest books are *Courage & Craft: Writing Your Life into Story* and *The Show & Tell Lion*. She writes a weekly blog at http://www.writingtime.net. Barbara lives with her husband in Santa Monica, California, and in Twin Bridges, Montana.

THE ROAD TAKEN

Eileen Goudge

When I was sixteen, I wanted to become a dancer. There was just one problem: I have hips. This I was made painfully aware of when my gym teacher, a middle-aged woman with the body of a reticular python (imagine the love child of Popeye and Olive Oyl), took me aside after class one day. She gave me one of those confidential, just-between-us-girls looks, which, as a teenager, you dread getting from anyone over the age of consent and which, coming from a teacher, is roughly akin to walking in on your

265

parents naked. It went something like this: "I don't mean to embarrass you, dear, but just felt I *had* to bring this to your attention . . ." Then she leaned in to deliver the words that were to be both the start of a lifelong preoccupation with my derriere and the end to any aspirations I'd had to become the next Martha Graham. "Are you aware that you *jiggle from behind*?" Red-faced, I managed to sputter in reply, "Well, um . . . no." Not one to snack on Yoo-Hoos or indulge in late-night binging, I was the same size 8 I'd always been. Yet I felt vaguely guilty somehow, as if I had been caught cheating on an exam. My gym teacher had a simple solution, however. "What I would suggest, dear, is a girdle."

I couldn't quite envision myself leaping around onstage trussed in Playtex—or, worse, engaging in spirited duets with my bobbling behind—so I became a writer instead. This wasn't as much of a stretch as you might think. Both professions demand a large degree of flexibility—in the case of writers, bending the truth and creating plot twists—and both require you to express yourself in public, often in ways that might prove hazardous. But while dancers face the ubiquitous twisted ankle or pulled groin muscle, for writers those hazards can take a more insidious form. To be more precise: family and friends that don't always cotton to being fodder for the grist mill. In a novel I wrote while getting divorced (not something I would recommend), I described the husband in the book as being a bit of a stick-in-the-mud: Every night before bed, he would place the contents of his pocket on his dresser—wallet, keys, spare change, business-card holder—lining them up in the same precise way each time. After reading the book, my real-life husband was not pleased.

An even more dramatic example of this occurred while I was on tour promoting my first novel, *Garden of Lies*. In interviews with the press, I talked about having once been a welfare mother. And while this was factually true—at the age of twenty-one, divorced, with a baby son and no viable means of support, I had been forced to go on public assistance for a brief period; I'd even stood in line for government surplus food— my parents took exception to it. My mother's response was, "But you weren't a *real* welfare mother." Meaning that I wasn't a black or Hispanic high school dropout who'd been living in a ghetto with rats crawling over my bed.

It sparked quite the family feud, and for the longest time we didn't speak to one another. But all these years later, I have a better understanding of where they were coming from. The fact that a child of theirs had been on welfare was embarrassing to them. Even more embarrassing was that it had been in the newspaper. They felt they'd been made to look responsible, though I never once suggested they were to blame or even mentioned them in any of my interviews, except to praise them. Whatever mistakes they might have made in raising me, they hadn't forced me at gunpoint to marry the father of my child (in fact, they'd actively discouraged it), nor had they insisted that I drop out of college to do so. Any blame for that rested squarely on my shoulders. I'd made my bed and, rats or no rats, I was the one who'd had to lie in it. What my parents didn't seem to grasp was it had been that dark period in my life, as demoralizing as it was, that galvanized me in a way I'm not sure a kick in the pants, or even a bachelor's degree, would have.

I remember clearly the day I hit rock bottom. I'd sat waiting to see my social worker for the better part of the afternoon, my baby fussing on my lap, only to be told as the office was closing to come back the next day. Returning home, I felt utterly dehumanized, a number on a docket rather than a person who might have had something better to do than cool her heels in a waiting room all day. I was sharing an apartment with my younger sister at the time. We lived upstairs from our landlord,

THE FACE IN THE MIRROR

who'd insisted we call him "Uncle" Ted.* We were so poor we couldn't even afford to have a phone installed, so we had to go to Uncle Ted's every time we needed to make a call. The problem with that, aside from the inconvenience, was that our landlord was in the habit of flashing us. He'd wait until we'd dialed and were more or less a captive audience, then out would come his wing-wang. Normally, this would've been grounds for arrest, or at the very least a good excuse to find another place to live. But the rent was cheap and the location ideal—a ten-minute bike ride from downtown (I didn't own a car, either)—so, being as he was otherwise harmless, I solved this by simply removing my glasses while making calls, thus reducing any peripheral distractions to a flesh-colored blur.

On that day when I hit rock bottom, I took stock of the situation: I had no job and no prospects. I was at the mercy of my landlord and his performing monkey of an organ. My diet consisted of reconstituted milk, bread from the day-old bakery, and government cheese, mixed in with whatever fruits and veggies I could scrounge. I couldn't even afford Pampers; I had to haul my baby's cloth diapers on the back of my bike to the laundromat. If I didn't find a way out of this hole, and soon, I knew I was in danger of its becoming a way of life, as opposed to a temporary solution. After indulging in an Itzhak Perlman–worthy solo on the world's smallest violin, accompanied by a bottle of Matteus wine someone had given me, I threw off the bonds of self-pity and made a mental list of possibilities: I could become a high-class hooker (scratch). I could go back to being a secretary (double scratch). I could get married again (first I'd have to find a husband, and in Santa Cruz, California, in the early seventies, the prospects were limited to stoners, surfers, counter-culture dropouts, and grad students at

---

*pseudonym

the university, most of whom were all of the above). Or—here I took a deep breath—I could become a writer. In school, my writings had earned praise from my teachers. One of my poems had even won third prize in a statewide contest. I felt I had the potential to become, if not the next John Steinbeck, then certainly the next Carolyn Keene. Also, this was a career that would require very little cash outlay.

Newly energized, I set about acquiring a typewriter. I couldn't afford to buy one, not even a used one, so I went next door to see if there was one I could borrow. I'd never met my neighbor—I'd only seen him through our window, which looked directly into his apartment, a slight, owl-eyed man whom my sister and I had dubbed Clock Man because you could set your clock by his routines—but I'd heard he was a professor and fig-ured I had a better chance of scoring office equipment than I would, say, a cup of flour. Luckily, my hunch proved correct: He just so happened to have an old Royal kicking around that he wasn't using, which he said he'd be happy to loan me. Well, maybe happy is too strong a word. I think he was more aston-ished than anything by this stranger who'd shown up at his door looking to borrow a typewriter when, by all appearances (remember, he had just as clear a view into *my* apartment as I did into his), she didn't even own a desk.

Clock Man was right about the desk. Our living room fur-niture was limited to an old sofa and chair inherited from the previous tenants. Not to be deterred, I plunked the Royal down on the carpet and began hammering away at the keys, heedless of any permanent damage I might be inflicting on my spine as this became my daily regime. My first efforts were aimed at the confession market. I don't know if it's still the case, but back then confession magazines paid by the word—twenty cents, I believe it was. I'd become fixated on the idea, imagining my borrowed typewriter a slot machine from which fistfuls of quarters tumbled with each typewritten page that scrolled off its carriage. An apt analogy, as it turned out: It wasn't long before I learned that the odds of a wannabe free-lance writer getting published are roughly on par with those in a Las Vegas casino (though I think you'd have better luck at the roulette tables). But by then I was hooked.

I remember my first story well. It was titled "Married Seven Years and Still a Virgin." I have no idea where I got the idea; all I know is that the story couldn't have been any good. But, of course, I was far less discerning then, so I promptly mailed it off to *Modern Romance*, confident of a speedy sale. Some weeks later it arrived back with a note clipped to it—nothing like the glowing comments my teachers used to scribble at the top of my essays, this was a form letter basically saying thanks but no thanks. This quickly became the story of my life: I would send out articles and short stories by the dozen, like a shipwrecked sailor frantically stuffing messages into bottles in the hope of being rescued, only to have them drift back to shore, one by one, on the tide of self-addressed stamped envelopes that washed up in my mailbox each day. It was many stamps and reams of paper later before I got so much as a nibble. My first sale was for a short piece that was published in the *National Star*, for which I received the princely sum of twenty dollars.

I wanted to frame the check, but I needed the money, so I framed a Xerox of it instead.

Over the next five or six years, I went on to publish many more articles and stories. Eventually, this led to my writing a novel. Like with my first efforts at short fiction, it wasn't a very good one, I'm afraid. It was an attempt to cash in on the then-popular genre of Gothic novels, and the best I can say about it is that it wasn't very long. Suffice it to say, the bad guy dies from inhaling the smoke from a pile of smoldering poison ivy. In retrospect, I realize I was lucky not to have found a publisher, as such early efforts have been known to haunt authors later in their career. To this day, it remains moldering in a box in my storage facility, where it belongs.

I learned from it, though. And eventually this led to my publishing a number of young adult novels. That was followed by my first adult hardcover, *Garden of Lies*, which went on to become a *New York Times* best seller. I remember the day I learned that it had hit what's known in the industry as The List. I had just come off my book tour. Earlier in the week, movie rights had been optioned for an ABC miniseries. To top it off, I had the entire front window of the B. Dalton on Fifth Avenue. I recall vividly standing on the sidewalk and gazing in wonder at the pyramids of books, a huge poster of the novel's distinctive green cover at the center, and feeling as if I'd truly arrived. I was no longer the welfare mom standing in line for surplus food, or the wannabe writer garnering more rejection slips than sales. I'd achieved the goal I'd set for myself.

The trouble was, I couldn't let it rest at that. When the book fell off The List after eight weeks, I grew depressed and began to fret. Why wasn't it still flying off store shelves? Was my publisher not doing enough to promote it? Were readers not generating enough word-of-mouth? When the final tally came in—an astounding number for a first novel—I wanted to know why it hadn't sold even *more* copies. Conversely, I was also terrified that my next book wouldn't live up to its success. A fear that proved justified. *Such Devoted Sisters*, which debuted a year and a half later, sold in the same numbers and even briefly hit the *Times* list, but was considered a "disappointment" because the publisher had put out twice as many copies. At this, I became *seriously* depressed. I didn't take into account that the book had come out at Christmastime, when it was most likely to get lost in the shuffle, or that its publication had coincided with death threats to the publisher, in the wake of the furor over Salman Rushdie's *Satanic Verses*. (It's pretty hard to concentrate on your job when there's a fatwa out on you and bomb-sniffing dogs are patrolling the office as you're trying to conduct business.) I was convinced I was a failure. In my mind, I was back where I'd started: hunched over the old typewriter on the floor, churning out stuff that nobody was going to want to read.

I was married to my agent then and had spent enough time around other writers to know I wasn't alone in this. There was the best-selling novelist, who after weeks in the number one slot on the *Times* list, fell into a funk when his book slipped to number two. And the British horror novelist, wildly popular in the UK, who fired his agent because his books weren't selling in the United States. My favorite was the writer of women's fiction who wanted to shoot herself (or someone else) because the advance for her second novel, though still in the high six figures, wasn't quite as hefty as for her first. Was there ever a point where you could sit back and savor your success, as you would a fine cabernet? When you didn't look at every failure through a magnifying glass? Sure, I thought. The day you were selling in such huge numbers that nothing could touch you. Bad reviews? They would slide right off instead of sticking like spillage from the *Exxon Valdez*. A slight dip in sales? Not a problem, when there were already millions of your titles in print worldwide. Even a fatwa wouldn't seem so terrible in light of being number one on the best-seller list.

I redoubled my efforts, leaving no stone unturned when it came to publicizing each title. I grew more savvy, as far as pub dates and print runs were concerned; I actively courted book-sellers. I even baked brownies and sent them to the sales reps— all forty of them (I was scraping brownies off the ceiling by the end of it). All because I was convinced that if I just tried hard enough, wrote fast enough, smiled at the right people, I, too, would one day occupy the lofty realm to which I aspired.

What happened instead was that I got older. And wiser, I hope. After I turned fifty, it occurred to me, in a very real sense, that the road I was on wasn't limitless, that there was a room at the Motel Six up ahead registered in my name. I don't mean to sound fatalistic. I'm in good health and don't expect to reach the end of that road anytime soon. But still. There it was: the realization that I wasn't going to live forever. Which led me to ponder the eternal question: What more did I want out of life? Was my happiness inextricably bound to the fulfillment of my expectations, or was it the other way around— did my expectations have my happiness in a bind?

I concluded, much to my dismay, that it was the latter: I was slowly being strangled by my own hand.

This all coincided with my falling in love. No, not with another man—I'm happily married to the love of my life whom I met, in a novel-worthy twist, while he was interviewing me over the phone for his radio show—but with an island in the Pacific Northwest. For some years, my husband and I had been taking our summer vacations on this island, dreaming of the day we would one day build a house there. Shortly after I had my epiphany, we bought property and subsequently sold our carriage house in Manhattan. We moved into an apartment a third the size of our old place and put the money we'd banked into building what will eventually be our retirement home. In the process, I found, to my surprise, that I preferred living in a smaller place. For one thing, I no longer felt compelled to work quite so hard. Don't get me wrong—I still work hard, just not to the point of being in danger of wandering, bleary-eyed, into the path of an oncoming bus. But in downsizing my lifestyle, I was also whittling away at my dream of being able to easily afford that lifestyle. This gave me pause, until I decided that it was silly to kill myself trying to achieve something that wouldn't make me any more content than I already was.

There's a fine line between happiness and contentment. The way I see it, happiness is quite often wrapped up in those peak moments: falling in love, having a baby, landing the dream job or promotion . . . or having the book you write wind up on the best-seller list. Contentment, on the other hand, is more of an everyday thing: the quiet moment at the start of the day when you sit on the porch with a cup of tea and watch the sun rise; getting lost in a good book; making a pie from blackberries you picked; curling up next to your honey to watch *Casablanca*, which never gets old even though you're seeing it for the umpteenth time; the feeling you get tucking your child in at night, freshly bathed and smelling the way heaven must. If I am to measure my life in such moments, I am already rich beyond compare. Anything more would be just the icing on the cake.

I go on striving because I can't *not* strive: My husband likes to joke that I didn't come equipped with a shut-off valve. But I no longer feel like a failure when I fall short of my goals. Nor do I fail to recognize the achievements I might once have downplayed, even if they aren't 100 percent of what I'd hoped for. I make time where I once would have said I was too busy. Time to take a walk or to try some of those recipes in my bulging clippings file . . . or break bread with a friend. I was reminded of the importance of this just recently, when a friend and his wife were visiting from out of town. I was on deadline, so I considered postponing our planned get-together until the next time they were in town. But in the end, knowing that he was battling cancer (which we all thought was in remission), I made time and cooked them a lovely dinner. And I'm very glad I did because he died a little more than a month later. Now, instead of regrets, I will always have the memory of our last, delightful dinner together to cherish.

Until it's time for me to pen the final The End, I want to be a guest at my own feast. I want to raise the proverbial glass and toast a life well lived, if not perfectly realized. To be grateful for the friends I brought to the table and the bounty before me. To throw my arms up and my head back and dance in celebration, mindless of any parts of my anatomy that might be dancing, too.

EILEEN GOUDGE began her publishing career as a penniless writer, eking out a living with the *Sweet Valley High* series. When she sold the *New York Times* best-selling *Garden of Lies*, her life changed dramatically. Her many novels include the recent *Woman in Red* and *Domestic Affairs*. Her cookbook, *Something Warm from the Oven*, was met with great acclaim. All twelve of her best-selling novels, including *One Last Dance*, *Garden of Lies*, *Such Devoted Sisters*, *Blessing in Disguise*, *Trail of Secrets*, and *Thorns of Truth*, are available as books on tape. Movie rights for *Woman in Red* were recently optioned by Lifetime. Eileen and her husband, Sandy Kenyon, the entertainment reporter for WABC, live in New York City. Her Web site is http://www.eileengoudge.com.

ACKNOWLEDGMENTS

For me, the thrill of creating an anthology is not so much the sale of the book to a publisher but the arrival of essays. As each e-mail appears with its precious attachment, I feel as if it's my birthday and I'm being blessed with a wonderful gift. I quickly shift into my routine: download the essay, print it out, prepare a mug of Irish tea, then settle into the sofa for a good read. I have an editing pen in hand, but I become so captivated that I forget to use it and must begin from the top. With every read, I experience a sense of awe that such gifted and generous authors have entrusted their work to me. Therefore, authors, I thank you first: Aviva Layton, Leon Whiteson, Lee Chamberlin, Barbara Abercrombie, Aimee Liu, Margot Duxler, Michael Bader, Sandra Gulland, Jane Ganahl, Alan Dershowitz, Christine O'Hagan, Laurie Stone, Richard Toon, Eileen Goudge, Kathi Kamen Goldmark, Malachy McCourt, Nancy Weber, Beverly Donofrio, and Joyce Maynard. This book sings with the music of your lives and I thank you with great affection.

At Prometheus, my thanks to editor Linda Regan for believing in this project and giving the authors the leeway to address the question of *Who am I?* in our own personal, and not always predictable, ways. And to publicist Jill Maxick for your enthusiastic support in the marketing of this book. Thanks also to Christine Kramer, Joe Gramlich, and Marcia Rogers for your expertise and support.

To dear friends and readers Masha Hamilton, Caroline Leavitt, Regina Anavy, and Sandra Gulland, what would I do without your unwavering encouragement? Thank you so much.

To my family, my loving thanks for your patience and for sharing my joy.

Thanks to the Sandra Dijkstra Literary Agency for your support with this project.

No one could ask for a wiser, kinder, wittier, more astute agent than Jill Marsal of the Marsal Lyon Literary Agency. What I do, I do better, knowing that you are nearby.